THE ILLUSTRATED MULTIPLAN® BOOK
(Version 2.0)

Russell A. Stultz

Wordware Publishing, Inc.
Dallas • London

Library of Congress Cataloging in Publication Data

Stultz, Russell Allen.
The illustrated Multiplan book.

Includes index.
1. Multiplan (Computer program). 2. Business—Data processing. I. Title.
HF5548.4M74S79 1986 005.36'9 86-13164
ISBN 0-915381-91-5

Interior Design — **Russell A. Stultz**
Production Manager — **Dianne Stultz**
Art Director — **Alan McCuller**
Manufacturing Manager — **Linda Davis**

1506 Capital Avenue
Plano, Texas 75074

Printed in the United States of America

ISBN 0-915381-91-5

10 9 8 7 6 5 4 3 2 1

All inquiries for volume purchases of this book should be addressed to Wordware Publishing, Inc. at the above address. Telephone inquiries may be made by calling (214) 423-0090.

Contents

Recommended Learning Sequence

Preface

About Electronic Worksheets Electronic worksheets, often called *spreadsheets*, have been around for several years. Even early, relatively primitive worksheets were a godsend to business managers, financial planners, cost estimators, and the like. And like most products, these powerful software tools continue to get better with age as new, advanced features are continually being added.

The family of financial planning software is constantly ranked in the top one or two of business software applications packages being purchased today. And rightfully so. Electronic worksheets are easy to use, versatile, and able to make you, the user, extremely productive.

The book describes the Microsoft(R) Multiplan(R) electronic worksheet. As a user of six different brands of worksheets, I believe Multiplan to be one of the finest on the market. It is one of the easiest electronic worksheets to learn. Its large repertoire of capabilities makes it an excellent choice for the serious electronic worksheet user.

I've personally used Multiplan for cost estimating, project planning, financial analysis, and many other purposes. I've included worksheet "setups," referred to as *templates*, in this book as models that you can use to solve problems of your own. If you're not sure how a command can be used to solve a financial problem, you can refer to the appropriate *module* within this book to see one or more typical illustrations.

About Illustrated Books As a classroom instructor of many kinds of microcomputer software applications, I find myself constantly searching for good, authoritative sources of information. This includes books that can help me learn and that are ready-made to help me teach others — ones that get at the "heart" of the information fast, that teach principles through practice.

That's how the Illustrated Dictionary series got it's beginning; it was devised to provide quick, easy-to-understand, well-illustrated information about an often complicated application.

The format lets you find the area of interest quickly. A description, applications, and step-by-step illustrations are provided. This combination gets results. It provides both quick answers and models that help solve real problems. You'll find that the Illustrated approach goes beyond standard documentation and books that treat software theoretically or in broad and sometimes vague terms.

I'm pleased to see that the series has gained wide acceptance by a large group of users. I've heard from classroom teachers, professional users, students, and "buffs" who are all using books from the series to fulfill specific needs of their own. I hope readers continue to enjoy using this series of books as much as I've enjoyed writing it.

Russell A. Stultz

Module 1

ABOUT THIS BOOK

INTRODUCTION

This book describes Microsoft® Corporation's Multiplan® Electronic Worksheet program. It shows how you can use Multiplan in the office and home, and presents detailed information about the many Multiplan commands; each command is accompanied by examples.

The book is designed for a broad range of users. It is for beginning users who wish to learn the Multiplan program from scratch. It is for intermediate and advanced users as a quick reference that contains examples of Multiplan commands. And finally, it is for the classroom instructor as an instructionally designed electronic worksheet textbook.

The Multiplan program is a sophisticated piece of software, yet it's easy to learn and use. You'll find that the versatility of an electronic worksheet becomes clear within a matter of an hour or two of practice. You'll also find that worksheets are fun to use. It's easy to enter text (or *labels*), numbers, and arithmetic expressions (or *equations*). Answers to problems appear instantly. And you can tap even greater analytical power as you experiment with new, advanced commands.

To prove to yourself how easy Multiplan is to use, you might want to jump over to Module 2 and go through the sample session with your computer. Here, you'll set up a simple electronic worksheet, enter several sets of numbers, and watch Multiplan give quick, accurate answers.

Module 2 is for you if you're an adventurous person who likes to "dive in." Once you've experienced a straightforward worksheet session, you'll have the foundation necessary to tackle the heavy stuff with relative ease.

ORGANIZATION

This book is organized into small, easy-to-read *modules*. These modules include descriptions, applications, and illustrations that provide insight into ways in which Multiplan can be used to solve practical, everyday problems. Literally hundreds of examples are presented in the Description, Applications, and Typical Operation sections of the modules.

These examples can be used as models from which to design applications of your own. The working examples let you experiment with Multiplan commands, taking the mystery out of what might otherwise be a technical obscurity. In addition to conducting "hands-on" experiments, you'll probably find yourself having a lot of fun, because Multiplan is a delightfully enjoyable program to operate.

With the exception of Modules 1 through 4, most of the modules in this book contain information that pertains to specific Multiplan commands or families of functions.

This module provides information about the book and briefly describes what kind of equipment is required to operate the Multiplan program.

Module 2 introduces you to Multiplan. It describes the term *electronic worksheet*, lists key sequences used by Multiplan, and walks you through two sample Multiplan sessions. You'll not only discover how Multiplan commands are used; you also can follow the sample session using your computer.

In addition to actually using some of the basic Multiplan commands, you'll prepare and save two sample Multiplan worksheets. By the time you've completed Module 2, the power of Multiplan will be apparent, because you'll have demonstrated how electronic worksheets are used to solve common, everyday problems.

Module 3 provides an overview of the structure of the Multiplan worksheet. It also contains information about how Multiplan is used to transfer financial information into files for use within word processed documents.

Module 4 contains a recommended sequence for learning (or teaching) Multiplan. As you work your way through this book, you can check off the modules you've completed. The sequence is arranged in a simple-to-complex order and can be modified to fit any classroom curriculum. If you're a teacher, you may wish to use Module 4 as a curriculum design aid.

Modules 5 through 26 describe and illustrate the Multiplan commands. The commands are arranged in alphabetical order, as in a dictionary, for easy reference. Of course you'll want to use the sequence outlined in Module 4 for learning.

Appendixes A through F provide a quick reference for Multiplan commands and operators. This information makes an excellent quick reference resource for finding information about specific commands.

Appendix G provides control key information for a variety of computer systems on which Multiplan operates.

Appendix H is provided for both classroom and self-teaching situations. It contains Multiplan exercises. If you're a classroom instructor, you may wish to include these exercises in student assignments. If you're learning Multiplan on your own, the exercises may be a good way to check yourself to see what you've learned about a command. If you can answer the questions, you're ready to move on to the next module in the learning sequence.

HARDWARE AND SOFTWARE REQUIREMENTS

The Multiplan program operates with most popular microcomputers. It originally was released for Microsoft's MS-DOS operating system, which is compatible with microcomputers using Intel's 8086 through 80386 series of microprocessors. It has since been modified to operate on several other machines. For example, Multiplan operates on microcomputers using the popular 8-bit 8080 and Z80 family of microprocessors. Multiplan is also available for 6502- and 6510-based microcomputers such as machines in the Apple II series, Commodore 64/128's, the Apple Macintosh, and several others.

To realize all the benefits of Multiplan, your computer should be equipped with at least 128-kilobytes of random access memory for version 2.0 or 64 kilobytes for versions released prior to 2.0.

You'll also want a printer. If you have a dot matrix printer that features compressed printing (16 or 17 characters per inch), all the better. The compressed print feature lets you print 132-character-wide documents on 8½-by-11-inch paper. Many daisy wheel printers also feature 15-character-per-inch printing, which can also be used to squeeze relatively wide worksheets on a standard letter-sized sheet of paper.

WHAT YOU SHOULD KNOW

You should be familiar with your computer, its keyboard, and the commands available on your operating system. Because most computers use either MS- or PC-DOS or CP/M, it is assumed that you know how to list a directory of files on your diskettes (or hard disks), format a disk, and copy, rename, and delete files. You should also know how to install Multiplan. Get out the Multiplan manual and go through the installation process before beginning Module 2. If you're familiar with your operating system and have installed (configured) Multiplan for your computer, you're ready to begin.

Module 2

MULTIPLAN OVERVIEW AND SAMPLE SESSION

INTRODUCTION

This module describes the term *electronic worksheet*, and presents information about ways in which Multiplan can be used to solve everyday problems. Two sample Multiplan sessions are included in which you're guided through the creation, data entry, filing, and retrieval of a typical worksheet.

THE ELECTRONIC WORKSHEET

Before starting our Multiplan session, a few explanations about electronic worksheets, the kinds of information they use, and some basic definitions are in order. We all keep financial information of some kind on either a ruled tablet, graph paper, or plain paper with hand-drawn vertical and horizontal lines. Generally, we have descriptive information down the left side and across the top of the sheet. Example 1 looks like the kind of thing many of us use to keep personal financial information.

Example 1 A Typical Worksheet

1	Description/Month	Jan	Feb	Mar	Apr	May	Jun	Totals
2	Take-Home Pay	1500	1750	1750	1750	1750	1750	10250
3	House Payment	424	424	424	424	424	424	2544
4	Car Payment	108	108	108	108	108	108	648
5	Groceries	280	227	265	301	284	302	1659
6	Gas	32	37	35	29	31	28	192
7	Water	29	27	31	47	52	49	235
8	Electricity	184	196	174	152	105	97	908
9	Gasoline & Oil	89	108	94	87	96	110	584
10	Clothing	94	35	26	87	49	164	455
11	Repairs/Upkeep	84	20	0	0	154	0	258
12	Medical Expenses	35	0	0	225	0	0	260
13	Insurance	75	75	75	75	75	75	450
14	Entertainment	50	50	50	50	50	50	300
15	Bal. for Savings	16	433	468	165	322	343	1747

An equivalent Multiplan display of Example 1 is shown in Example 2.

Example 2 The Typical Worksheet in Multiplan

	1	2	3	4	5	6	7	8
1	Description/Month	Jan	Feb	Mar	Apr	May	Jun	Totals
2	Take-Home Pay	1500	1750	1750	1750	1750	1750	10250
3	House Payment	424	424	424	424	424	424	2544
4	Car Payment	108	108	108	108	108	108	648
5	Groceries	280	227	265	301	284	302	1659
6	Gas	32	37	35	29	31	28	192
7	Water	29	37	31	47	52	49	245
8	Electricity	184	196	174	152	105	97	908
9	Gasoline & Oil	89	108	94	87	96	110	584
10	Clothing	94	35	26	87	49	164	455
11	Repairs/Upkeep	84	20	0	0	154	0	258
12	Medical Expenses	35	0	0	225	0	0	260
13	Insurance	75	75	75	75	75	75	450
14	Entertainment	50	50	50	50	50	50	300
15	Bal. for Savings	16	433	468	165	322	343	1747

ROWS, COLUMNS, AND CELLS Notice that the information is arranged in rows and columns. The columns are numbered 1 through 8; the rows 1 through 15. The intersection of row 1 and column 1 is expressed as R1C1 (for row 1 column 1). In Multiplan, row-column intersections are referred to as *cells*. Using this language, cell R5C3 contains grocery expenses for the month of February, while cell R8C4 contains electricity expenses for March.

WORKSHEET SIZE The original Multiplan worksheet was 255 rows long and 63 columns wide. Multiplan version 2.0 is 4095 rows long and 255 columns wide. In either version, you can't see the entire worksheet at once. You can see only 20 rows and about seven 10-character-wide columns. Column widths can be made narrower so that you can view more of the worksheet. As you can see, viewing Multiplan on your screen is like looking through a window at a portion of a large worksheet.

ALPHABETICAL, NUMERICAL, AND FORMULA ENTRIES You can enter three types of information into a cell. First, you can enter text, like the row and column headings shown in our example. These entries are referred to as *Alpha* entries. You can also use numbers, punctuation marks, underscores, and other symbols within Alpha entries, but they are treated as text. Alpha entries are usually used as column or row headings (or *labels*), rules, notes, and the like. Unless you change the position of Alpha entries with Multiplan's Format command, they are displayed flush left in their cell location.

Second, you can enter numbers, like the dollar amounts in our example. These entries are a subset of the Value command, which allows entry of either numbers or formulas. Numbers within Value cells are in many forms, including whole numbers (integers), decimal values, percentages, dollars and cents, and bars made up of asterisks. Either positive or negative number values are possible.

Finally, there are formulas. Formulas are entered using Multiplan's Value command. As you might expect, formulas are simply mathematical expressions used to add, subtract, multiply, divide, sum, average, and so on. In addition to being able to perform mathematical computations, you can use cell names in your formulas.

ABSOLUTE AND RELATIVE CELL REFERENCES The concept of absolute and relative cell reference is important. Several examples are used to describe cell referencing. If you are already familiar with cell referencing, skip to the Multiplan Control Keys paragraph; otherwise, spend a few minutes studying absolute and relative cell notation.

Cells are referred to in *absolute* terms — that is, you can refer to specific cells by row and column number in the form RnCn, where *n* is a number. Cells are also referred to in *relative* terms. "Relative to what?" you may ask. Relative to the location of the cell in which a formula is entered. Notice the following diagram.

	Col 1	**Col 2**	**Col 3**
Row 1	R[– 1]C[– 1]	R[– 1]C	R[– 1]C[+ 1]
Row 2	RC[– 1]	R2C2	RC[+ 1]
Row 3	R[+ 1]C[– 1]	R[+ 1]C	R[+ 1]C[+ 1]
Row 4	R[+ 2]C[– 1]	R[+ 2]C	R[+ 2]C[+ 1]

Row 2 column 2 (R2C2) is an absolute cell reference. When R2C2 is used as a basis, we can refer to cell R1C2 as row less 1 (R[– 1]), same column (C). This is R[– 1]C in relative notation. R2C3 is referred to as same row (R) plus one column [+ 1], which is RC[+ 1]. The other relative references are shown in the diagram. Moving down and to the right (to higher-numbered rows and columns) is " + "; moving up and to the left (to lower-numbered rows and columns) is " – ." Consider the following examples of absolute and relative cell references.

If you want to enter the sum of the "Take-Home Pay" row (R2) into cell R2C8 of Example 1 (where C8 is the "Totals" column), you can use the Value command to enter the expression

R2C2 + R2C3 + R2C4 + R2C5 + R2C6 + R2C7

in cell R2C8. An alternative formula could be

SUM(R2C2:R2C7) or SUM(R2C2:7)

where the colon (:) designates the full range of cells between R2C2 and R2C7. The second expression says "Sum the cells in row 2 beginning with column 2 and ending with column 7." Both expressions are valid and have the same meaning.

The SUM operator works with the cell range in the following parenthetical expression. (More about mathematical expressions in Module 3.) Both of these examples demonstrate absolute cell notation, where specific cell positions are used.

The same answer is derived using relative cell notation. Taking the first example, the formula

SUM(RC[– 6]:RC[– 1])

in cell R2C8 adds the range of cells in the same row beginning with the sixth column to the left (C[– 6]) and ending with one column to the left (C[– 1]).

A formula that uses relative values in the "Bal. for Savings" row (R15) is

R[– 13]C – SUM(R[– 12]C:R[– 1]C)

which may be stated as "the value in the cell 13 rows above in this column less the sum of the values in this column from 12 rows above through one row above."

As a final illustration of relative cell notation, a portion of Example 2 is shown with formulas in the "Totals" column.

Example 3   The Typical Worksheet (Partial) Showing Relative Formulas

	1	2	...	7	8
1	"Description/Month"	"Jan"	...	"Jun"	"Totals"
2	"Take-Home Pay"	1500	...	1750	SUM(RC[-6]:RC[-1])
3	"House Payment"	424	...	424	SUM(RC[-6]:RC[-1])
4	"Car Payment"	108	...	108	SUM(RC[-6]:RC[-1])
5	"Groceries"	280	...	302	SUM(RC[-6]:RC[-1])
6	"Gas"	32	...	28	SUM(RC[-6]:RC[-1])
7	"Water"	29	...	49	SUM(RC[-6]:RC[-1])
8	"Electricity"	184	...	97	SUM(RC[-6]:RC[-1])
9	"Gasoline & Oil"	89	...	110	SUM(RC[-6]:RC[-1])
10	"Clothing"	94	...	164	SUM(RC[-6]:RC[-1])
11	"Repairs/Upkeep"	84	...	0	SUM(RC[-6]:RC[-1])
12	"Medical Expenses"	35	...	0	SUM(RC[-6]:RC[-1])
13	"Insurance"	75	...	75	SUM(RC[-6]:RC[-1])
14	"Entertainment"	50	...	50	SUM(RC[-6]:RC[-1])
15	"Bal. for Savings"	R[-13]C-SUM (R[-12]C:R[-1]C)	...	R[-13]C-SUM (R[-12]C:R[-1]C)	R[-13]C-SUM (R[-12]C:R[-1]C)

MULTIPLAN CONTROL KEYS

The keys that control such things as cursor movement and editing vary with the keyboard being used. Table 2-1 provides some common key sequences that are used with Multiplan for cursor control and editing. The reference is the name by which the command is called in this book. For terminals other than the IBM-PC or compatibles, refer to Appendix G.

Table 2-1 Multiplan Control Keys

Function	*Reference*	*Typical Key Sequences*	
Cell pointer to upper left corner of worksheet	Home	Home	Ctrl-Q
Cell pointer right one cell	Right Arrow	Right Arrow	Ctrl-D
Cell pointer left one cell	Left Arrow	Left Arrow	Ctrl-S
Cell pointer up one cell	Up Arrow	Up Arrow	Ctrl-E
Cell pointer down one cell	Down Arrow	Down Arrow	Ctrl-X
Cell pointer to bottom right corner of worksheet	End	End	Ctrl-Z
Cell pointer to next unlocked cell	Next Cell	F2	Ctrl-F
Down one screen	Page Down	Pg Dn	
Up one screen	Page Up	Pg Up	
Right one screen	Page Right	Ctrl-Right Arrow	
Left one screen	Page Left	Ctrl-Left Arrow	
Cell pointer to next window	Next Window	F1	Ctrl-W
Recalculate	Recalc	F4	!
Help	Help	Alt-H	?
Next menu option	Tab or Space	Tab or Spacebar	Ctrl-I
Complete text or value entry Return	Return	Ctrl-M	
Cancel (or "undo") entry	Esc	Esc	Ctrl-C
Operate one step at a time	Single Step	Shift-F5	Ctrl-T
Jump to home window	Home Window	Ctrl-Home	
Expand entry	Expand	F6	:
Text Entry/Editing Keys:			
Cursor left one character	Char Left	F9	Ctrl-K
Cursor right one character	Char Right	F10	Ctrl-L
Cursor left one word	Word Left	F7	Ctrl-O
Cursor right one word	Word Right	F8	Ctrl-P
Delete character	Del	Del	
Delete char left	Back Space	Back Space	Ctrl-H
Edit macro	Edit Macro	F5	Ctrl-V
Insert cell reference	Reference	F3	@

Table 2-1 Multiplan Control Keys (Continued)

Command Line Entry Summary

Alpha entry (text, rules)	Alpha	A	Options (recalc., mute)	Options	O
Blank cell contents	Blank	B	Print (to printer or file)	Pront	P
Copy row or column	Copy	C	Quit (or exit Multiplan)	Quit	Q
Delete row or column	Delete	D	Sort column alphabetically or numerically	Sort	S
Edit cell entry	Edit	E			
Format	Format	F	Transfer (file operations)	Transfer	T
Goto specific cell	Goto	G	Value entry (numbers or formulas) also 0 - 9, =, (, +, or −	Value	V
Help information	Help	H			
Insert row or column	Insert	I			
Lock (protect) cell entry	Lock	L	Window (divide worksheet into segments)	Window	W
Move row or column	Move	M			
Name one or more cells	Name	N	External (use/link other worksheets)	Xternal	X

TIPS:

1. To enter text into a cell, always begin by pressing **Return** (if "Alpha" is highlighted) or by typing an A for Alpha. If you forget to do this and simply begin typing, Multiplan interprets the first key pressed as a command, not a text character.
2. When you are entering or editing text or values, pressing a cursor key moves the cell pointer, not the position of the cursor on the text entry line. Remember to always use the Right and Left Char or Word key sequences during text entry/editing.
3. If you "goof," simply press **Esc** and start over.
4. Refer to Table 3-1 in Module 3 for a complete table of commands.
5. If you wish to "blank" an unwanted entry, position the cell pointer to the unwanted cell and type **B** for Blank and press **Return**.

SAMPLE MULTIPLAN SESSIONS

Now that you have some worksheet terminology under your belt and know where to find control keys, it's time to jump in. Two sessions are included. The first is a simple one that lets you calculate your automobile's gasoline consumption. The second session computes pay rates. Each session takes you from the operating system prompt and walks you through worksheet creation, data entry, filing, and retrieval. You should have no trouble with the first session. If you find yourself having trouble with the second one, you may want to skip it and go directly to the recommended learning sequence (Module 4).

GASOLINE MILEAGE WORKSHEET In this sample session, you'll create a worksheet to compute your car's gas mileage. To compute gasoline mileage, divide the miles traveled by the gallons consumed. Therefore, you must record odometer readings and gasoline "fillups." The miles traveled are divided by the gasoline consumed to figure miles per gallon.

To illustrate the process, let's say that you fill your tank with an odometer reading of 32105 miles. At your next fillup, you pump 17.4 gallons of gasoline with an odometer reading of 32487. Your mileage is

$$(32487 - 32105)/17.4 = 382/17.4 = 21.95$$

To determine automobile performance from one period to another, you'll want to record the date as well. You may also want to check your average gas mileage, which is done by maintaining a cumulative record of miles traveled and gallons used.

Let's get started by activating Multiplan and designing a worksheet. To create the gasoline mileage worksheet, perform the following steps:

1. From the operating system prompt type **MP** and press **Return**.
2. Notice the Multiplan display; the word "Alpha" is highlighted on the status line.

```
#1     1        2        3        4        5        6        7
 1
 2
 3
 4
 5
 6
 7
 8
 9
10
11
12
13
14
15
16
17
18
19
20
COMMAND:Alpha Blank Copy Delete Edit Format Goto Help Insert Lock Move
        Name Options Print Quit Sort Transfer Value Window Xternal
Select option or type command letter
R1C1                                     100% Free       Multiplan:TEMP
```

3. Using the cursor control keys, move the cell pointer to the right and down to get the feel of moving around in a worksheet. The position of the cell pointer determines the point of text and numerical entry.

4. Press **Home** to move the cell pointer to R1C1.

NOTE
The following worksheet is created using steps 5 through 12.

```
        1         2         3         4        5
1 Date      Odometer  Miles     Gallons   MPG
2 --------------------------------------------------
3
4
5
6
7
8
9
```

5. Type **A**; notice that "ALPHA" is displayed in place of the status line followed by the cursor. Type **Date** and press **Return**; notice that "Date" is displayed in cell R1C1.
6. Move the cell pointer to cell R1C2, type **A Odometer**, and press **Return**. Notice that "Odometer" is displayed in cell R1C2.
7. Continue using the Alpha command to enter "Miles", "Gallons," and "MPG" in cells R1C3 through R1C5. If you have any trouble, review steps 5 and 6.
8. Move the cell pointer to R2C1, type **A** and ten hyphens, and press **Return**. Notice that a horizontal rule is displayed in cell R2C1.
9. Type **C R 4** for Copy Right 4 and press **Return**. Notice that the horizontal rule is copied; your worksheet should now look like the one shown above.
10. Move the cell pointer to cell R4C3 and enter the following keystrokes:

Keystroke	*Results*
V	VALUE:
Cell pointer to R4C2	VALUE: RC[-1]
-	VALUE: RC[-1]-
Cell pointer to R3C2	VALUE: RC[-1]-R[-1]C[-1]
Return	Completes formula entry

This formula computes the miles traveled from the "Odometer" column.

11. Copy the formula down 5 cells by typing **C D 5** and pressing **Return**.
12. Move the cell pointer to R4C5 and enter the following keystrokes:

Keystroke	*Results*
V	VALUE:
Cell pointer to R4C3	VALUE: RC[-2]

/	VALUE: RC[-2]/
Cell pointer to R4C4	VALUE: RC[-2]/RC[-1]
Return	Completes formula entry

This formula divides the miles traveled by the number of gallons to compute miles per gallon.

13. Copy the formula down 5 cells by typing **C D 5** and pressing **Return**.

14. Use the Alpha command to enter the dates in the "Date" column as shown in the following illustration.

	1	2	3	4	5
1	Date	Odometer	Miles	Gallons	MPG
2	-----------	----------	----------	----------	----------
3	10/21/84				
4	10/28/84		0		#DIV/0!
5	11/04/84		0		#DIV/0!
6	11/10/84		0		#DIV/0!
7			0		#DIV/0!
8			0		#DIV/0!
9			0		#DIV/0!

15. Enter the values shown in the "Odometer" and "Gallons" columns of the following illustration and notice the worksheet response.

	1	2	3	4	5
1	Date	Odometer	Miles	Gallons	MPG
2	-----------	----------	----------	----------	----------
3	10/21/84	32158			
4	10/28/84	32398	240	13.6	17.647059
5	11/04/84	32648	250	14.1	17.730496
6	11/10/84	32909	261	14.6	17.876712
7			-32909		#DIV/0!
8			0		#DIV/0!
9			0		#DIV/0!

16. This completes the worksheet; you can save it by typing **T S** for Transfer Save, entering a filename (like GAS.MP), and pressing **Return**. If you want to save the worksheet file on a disk in a drive other than the logged (or default) drive, prefix the filename with the drive designator (like B:GAS.MP).

17. After saving the worksheet, quit Multiplan by typing **Q** for Quit. This completes the first sample session.

PAY RATE CONVERSION TABLE A pay rate conversion table is developed in this session. You'll use commands for entering text, numbers, and formulas and for formatting cell widths and displaying numbers as dollars and cents. Then you'll save your work to a file and return to the operating system prompt. Next, you'll return to Multiplan and retrieve your saved file.

The pay rate conversion table worksheet computes several different factors. It converts hourly pay rates into weekly, monthly, and annual pay rates. It converts monthly pay rates into hourly, weekly, and annual pay rates. Finally, it converts wage increases expressed in dollars and cents to percentage increases. Formulas used for these processes are

Conversion	Formula
Hourly to weekly	40 X hourly rate
Hourly to monthly	40 X 52 X hourly rate/12
Hourly to annual	12 X monthly rate
Monthly to hourly	Monthly rate/173.3333
Monthly to weekly	Monthly rate X 12/52
Monthly to annual	12 X monthly rate
Amount of increase to percentage	Amount of increase/present rate

Once the worksheet is completed, you can enter hourly or monthly rates and Multiplan will automatically convert them for you. This type of worksheet is good for salary planning. If you feel as if you're getting over your head, move on to the recommended learning sequence in Module 4. You may want to familiarize yourself with Module 3, so you'll know where to find Multiplan reference information.

To create the salary planning worksheet, insert your Multiplan diskette in disk drive A and perform the following steps:

1. From the operating system prompt type **MP** and press **Return**.
2. Notice the Multiplan display; the word "Alpha" is highlighted on the status line.
3. Using the cursor control keys, move the cell pointer to the right and down to get the feel of moving around in a worksheet. The position of the cell pointer determines the point of text and numerical entry.
4. Press **Home** to move the cursor to R1C1.
5. Type **A**; notice that "ALPHA" is displayed in place of the status line, followed by the cursor. Type **Description** and press **Return**; notice that the entire word doesn't fit in R1C1.
6. Type **F W 20** (no spaces) and press **Return**; notice that the width of column 1 increases to 20 characters.
7. Position the cell pointer to R1C2, type **A** for Alpha, then type **Current** and press **Right Arrow**.
8. Using the cursor keys to point to the proper cells, enter the following text in the cells as shown. (Don't type row and column numbers.)

```
                   1            2         3          4          5
 1 Description             Current  Amount of  Adjusted   Percent
 2                         Rate     Increase   Rate       Increase
```

9. Position the cell pointer to R3C1, type **A** for Alpha, type a horizontal rule using 20 hyphens, and press **Return**.

10. Copy the rule four cells to the right by typing **CR 4** and pressing **Return**; notice the prompt activity as you type. The rule is copied from R3C1 to R3C2 through R3C5. The top three rows should appear as follows.

```
                   1            2         3          4          5
 1 Description             Current  Amount of  Adjusted   Percent
 2                         Rate     Increase   Rate       Increase
 3 ------------------------------------------------------------
```

11. Position the cell pointer to R5C1 and type **C F** for Copy From; move the cell pointer to R3C1 and press **Return**. The rule at R3C1 is copied to R5C1.

12. Using your cursor keys to point to the appropriate cells and the Alpha command for text entry, type the text in column 1 until your worksheet looks like the following illustration.

```
                   1            2         3          4          5
 1 Description             Current  Amount of  Adjusted   Percent
 2                         Rate     Increase   Rate       Increase
 3 ------------------------------------------------------------
 4 Non-Exempt (Hourly)
 5 --------------------
 6 Hourly Rate
 7
 8 Weekly Rate
 9 Monthly Rate
10 Annual Salary
11
12 Exempt (Monthly)
13 --------------------         (Use Copy From, point to R5C1, and press Return)
14 Monthly Rate
15
16 Hourly Rate
17 Weekly Rate
18 Annual Salary
```

13. Using the Alpha command, type a space and nine hyphens in cell R7C2; then copy right one cell by typing **C R 1** and pressing **Return**.

14. Repeat step 13 with the cell pointer in cell R15C2. Your spreadsheet should appear as shown in the following illustration.

```
             1              2         3         4         5
 1 Description          Current  Amount of  Adjusted  Percent
 2                      Rate     Increase   Rate      Increase
 3 ------------------------------------------------------------
 4 Non-Exempt (Hourly)
 5 --------------------
 6 Hourly Rate
 7                      --------- ---------
 8 Weekly Rate
 9 Monthly Rate
10 Annual Salary
11
12 Exempt (Monthly)
13 --------------------
14 Monthly Rate
15                      --------- ---------
16 Hourly Rate
17 Weekly Rate
18 Annual Salary
```

15. Position the cell pointer to R8C2 and enter the following keystrokes:

Keystroke	*Results*
V	VALUE:
40*	VALUE: 40*
Cell pointer to R6C2	VALUE: 40*R[-2]C
Return	Completes formula entry

Notice that the formula "40*R[-2]C" appears on the status line for R8C2.

16. Position the cell pointer to R9C2 and enter the following keystrokes:

Keystroke	*Results*
V	VALUE:
40*52*	VALUE: 40*52*
Cell pointer to R6C2	VALUE: 40*52*R[-3]C
/12	VALUE: 40*52*R[-3]C/12
Return	Completes formula entry

Notice that the formula "40*52*R[-3]C/12" appears on the status line for R9C2.

17. Using the cursor keys and the Value command, type the rest of the formulas as shown. (These formulas are taken from the conversion table located at the beginning of this session.) The Value command is started by typing a number, **V**, or the = sign. The formulas only appear on the status line. Until numerical entries are made in step 25, zeros are displayed in the formula cells. Remember to use the cursor keys to point to cells. This automatically enters relative cell notation. (Don't type relative cell notation.) Some notation examples follow.

    R[-1]C designates one row up, same column.
    R[-2]C designates two rows up, same column.
    R[-3]C designates three rows up, same column.

Entries such as 40* (40 times) and /12 (divide by 12) are entered directly from the keyboard.

```
                  1                   2              3              4              5
 1 Description          Current        Amount of      Adjusted       Percent
 2                      Rate           Increase       Rate           Increase
 3 ----------------------------------------------------------------------------
 4 Non-Exempt (Hourly)
 5 --------------------
 6 Hourly Rate
 7                         ---------      ---------
 8 Weekly Rate          40*R[-2]C
 9 Monthly Rate         40*52*R[-3]C/12
10 Annual Salary        12*R[-1]C
11
12 Exempt (Monthly)
13 --------------------
14 Monthly Rate
15                         ---------      ---------
16 Hourly Rate          R[-2]C/173.3333
17 Weekly Rate          12*R[-3]C/52
18 Annual Salary        12*R[-4]C
```

18. Position the cell pointer to R6C4 and type **V** for Value, move the cell pointer to R6C2, type **+**, move the cell pointer to R6C3, and press **Return**. The formula "RC[– 2] + RC[– 1]" should appear on the status line.

19. Type the formulas in R8C4, R9C4, and R10C4 as shown in the following illustration using the cell pointer and the Value command.

```
                1              2              3              4              5
 1 Description        Current        Amount of      Adjusted       Percent
 2                    Rate           Increase       Rate           Increase
 3 ------------------------------------------------------------------------------
 4 Non-Exempt (Hourly)
 5 --------------------
 6 Hourly Rate                                      RC[-2]+RC[-1]
 7                       ---------      ---------
 8 Weekly Rate                   0                  40*R[-2]C
 9 Monthly Rate                  0                  40*52*R[-3]C/12
10 Annual Salary                 0                  12*R[-1]C
11
12 Exempt (Monthly)
13 --------------------
14 Monthly Rate
15                       ---------      ---------
16 Hourly Rate                   0
17 Weekly Rate                   0
18 Annual Salary                 0
```

20. Position the cell pointer to R14C4, type **C F** for Copy From, move the cell pointer to R6C4, and press **Return**.

21. Position the cell pointer to R8C4, type **C F** for Copy From, move the cell pointer to R8C2, type : (colon designates "range"), move the cell pointer to R10C2, and press **Return**. Notice that the full range of formulas from R8C2 through R10C2 is copied beginning at R8C4.

22. Position the cell pointer to R16C4, type **C F** for Copy From, move the cell pointer to cell R16C2, type :, move the cell pointer to R18C2, and press **Return**.

NOTE
To check your formulas, move the cell pointer to the cells containing formulas and review them on the status line.

```
                  1                2              3              4              5
 1 Description          Current        Amount of      Adjusted       Percent
 2                      Rate           Increase       Rate           Increase
 3 -----------------------------------------------------------------------------
 4 Non-Exempt (Hourly)
 5 --------------------
 6 Hourly Rate                                                   0
 7                        ---------      ---------
 8 Weekly Rate          40*R[-2]C       }              { 40*R[-2]C
 9 Monthly Rate         40*52*R[-3]C/12 }  COPIED->    { 40*52*R[-3]C/12
10 Annual Salary        12*R[-1]C       }              { 12*R[-1]C
11
12 Exempt (Monthly)
13 --------------------
14 Monthly Rate                                                  0
15                        ---------      ---------
16 Hourly Rate          R[-2]C/173.3333 }              { R[-2]C/173.3333
17 Weekly Rate          12*R[-3]C/52    }  COPIED->    { 12*R[-3]C/52
18 Annual Salary        12*R[-4]C       }              { 12*R[-4]C
```

23. Position the cell pointer to R6C5, type **V** for Value, move the cell pointer to R6C3, type **/** for Divide By, move the cell pointer to R6C2, and press **Return**. The formula "RC[– 2]/RC[– 3]" should be displayed on the status line.

24. Position the cell pointer to R14C5, type **C F** for Copy From, move the cell pointer to R6C5, and press **Return**. The completed worksheet should look like following illustration. Remember, formulas within cells only appear at the bottom left-hand corner of the screen. The message "#DIV/0!" is displayed in column 5.

```
                1                 2            3            4            5
 1 Description          Current      Amount of    Adjusted     Percent
 2                      Rate         Increase     Rate         Increase
 3 -------------------------------------------------------------------
 4 Non-Exempt (Hourly)
 5 --------------------
 6 Hourly Rate                                  RC[-2]+RC[-1]  RC[-2]/RC[-3]
 7                        ---------   ---------
 8 Weekly Rate          40*R[-2]C                 40*R[-2]C
 9 Monthly Rate         40*52*R[-3]C/12           40*52*R[-3]C/12
10 Annual Salary        12*R[-1]C                 12*R[-1]C
11
12 Exempt (Monthly)
13 --------------------
14 Monthly Rate                                 RC[-2]+RC[-1]  RC[-2]/RC[-3]
15                        ---------   ---------
16 Hourly Rate          R[-2]C/173.3333           R[-2]C/173.3333
17 Weekly Rate          12*R[-3]C/52              12*R[-3]C/52
18 Annual Salary        12*R[-4]C                 12*R[-4]C
```

25. The worksheet is complete except for entering numerical values in cells R6C2 (current hourly rate), R14C2 (current monthly rate), R6C3 (hourly rate amount of increase), and R14C3 (monthly rate amount of increase). You may now enter hourly and monthly rates and wage increases of your choosing to determine periodic wages and percentages of increases. You might try the numbers that follow to see if you've correctly entered your worksheet.

```
                   1              2         3         4         5
 1 Description          Current   Amount of Adjusted  Percent
 2                      Rate      Increase  Rate      Increase
 3 ------------------------------------------------------------
 4 Non-Exempt (Hourly)
 5 --------------------
 6 Hourly Rate              11.95         1     12.95  0.083682
 7                      --------- ---------
 8 Weekly Rate                478                 518
 9 Monthly Rate         2071.3333           2244.6667
10 Annual Salary            24856               26936
11
12 Exempt (Monthly)
13 --------------------
14 Monthly Rate              2000       200      2200       0.1
15                      --------- ---------
16 Hourly Rate          11.538464            12.69231
17 Weekly Rate          461.53846           507.69231
18 Annual Salary            24000               26400
```

26. To "spruce up" the worksheet, we'll use the Format command to center column headings, convert rates to dollars and cents notation, and change the percentage of increase to percent notation as follows:

   a. Position the cell pointer to R1C2 and type **F C** for Format Cell; notice that "R1C2" appears in the status line display.

   b. Type :, move the cell pointer to R2C5, press **Tab**, type **C** for Center, and press **Return**; notice that the column headings in columns 2 through 5 are centered.

   c. Position the cell pointer to R6C2 and type **F C**; notice that "R6C2" appears in the status line display.

   d. Type :, move the cell pointer to R18C4, press **Tab Tab**, type **$**, and press **Return**; notice that the numbers within the selected range of cells convert to dollars and cents.

   e. Position the cell pointer to R6C5 and type **F C** for Format Cell; notice that "R6C5" appears in the status line display.

   f. Type :, move the cell pointer to R14C5, press **Tab Tab**, type **%**, and press **Return**; notice that the numbers in column 5 convert to percent notation.

The final worksheet should appear as shown in the following illustration.

```
                     1             2          3          4         5
 1 Description             Current  Amount of  Adjusted  Percent
 2                           Rate    Increase    Rate    Increase
 3 --------------------------------------------------------------
 4 Non-Exempt (Hourly)
 5 --------------------
 6 Hourly Rate              $11.95      $1.00    $12.95         8%
 7                       --------- ---------
 8 Weekly Rate             $478.00              $518.00
 9 Monthly Rate           $2071.33             $2244.67
10 Annual Salary         $24856.00            $26936.00
11
12 Exempt (Monthly)
13 --------------------
14 Monthly Rate           $2000.00    $200.00  $2200.00        10%
15                       --------- ---------
16 Hourly Rate              $11.54               $12.69
17 Weekly Rate             $461.54              $507.69
18 Annual Salary         $24000.00            $26400.00
```

27. Now that the worksheet is created, you can save it to disk by typing **T S** for Transfer Save. Type a filename of eight characters or less, such as **PAYCHART.MP**, and press **Return**. If you wish to save the file to a diskette in drive B, prefix the filename with B:. Once **Return** is pressed, you'll notice disk drive activity as the worksheet is saved. Use of MP as an extension lets you know which files are Multiplan files. This is optional, but it is recommended to make it easier to identify Multiplan files in your disk directory.

28. To exit (or Quit) Multiplan operation after you have saved a worksheet, type **Q** for Quit. The system prompt appears.

29. To restart Multiplan without simultaneously loading a worksheet, you can type **MP** and press **Return**. When a blank worksheet is displayed, you can either begin creating a new worksheet or load an existing one. To load an existing worksheet, type **T L** for Transfer Load, then type the filename and press **Return**. If the worksheet file is located on another diskette, prefix the filename with a disk drive designator, such as B:FILENAME for drive B.

30. To load a file at startup, simply type **MP** followed by a space and the filename of the worksheet you want to load. Multiplan automatically loads the named worksheet during startup. Don't forget to prefix the filename with a disk drive designator, such as B:PAYCHART.MP, if the worksheet is on the diskette in drive B.

This concludes the sample session. If you successfully worked your way through the session and, in particular, if you understand most of the things you did, you'll have no trouble with the following modules in this book.

Module 3

MULITIPLAN COMMAND STRUCTURE AND OPERATORS

INTRODUCTION

This module provides an overview of the Multiplan command structure and lists mathematical and logical operators. This information can be used as a quick reference resource when you want to refresh your memory about primary and subordinate commands or operators. A brief discussion about how Multiplan can be used to produce financial information for use within word processed documents is also included.

WORKSHEET COMMAND LINE

Multiplan's command keys begin with *A* for Alpha and end with *X* for Xternal. With only a few exceptions, pressing a Multiplan command key displays a series of subordinate choices. This module provides an overview of the choices available within each function.

Appendix A lists the commands on the command lines, shows subordinate commands, and provides a brief description. Each of the commands is described in detail with examples in Modules 5 through 26.

Appendixes B through F list Multiplan functions, operators, and error messages. If you need a quick overview of a function or operator, refer to the appropriate appendix. Check the contents for specific appendix titles.

MERGING WORKSHEETS WITH WORD PROCESSED DOCUMENTS

The ability to merge the contents of a worksheet into a word processed document is extremely useful. Mathematical tables of all kinds can be "printed to a file" using Multiplan's Print command. Once the document is printed to the file, it is in ASCII form (standard data format), which can be read into word processors, such as WordStar, Newword, WordPerfect, Multimate, XYWRITE, or any other that handles or converts standard ASCII text files.

Once the worksheet is in the document, you can adjust such things as line spacing, margins, column and row text, and underscores and boldface using your text editing functions.

Business proposals often include financial information, such as cash flow information, breakeven analyses, and expense-to-revenue models. These are the kind of things that electronic worksheets do best. Therefore, once you've computed the data using a worksheet, you can print either part or all of the worksheet to a file, which in turn can be included in your proposal. The ability to print to file is discussed in greater detail in Module 20.

A replica of a blank worksheet is shown below. The various parts of the worksheet are labeled.

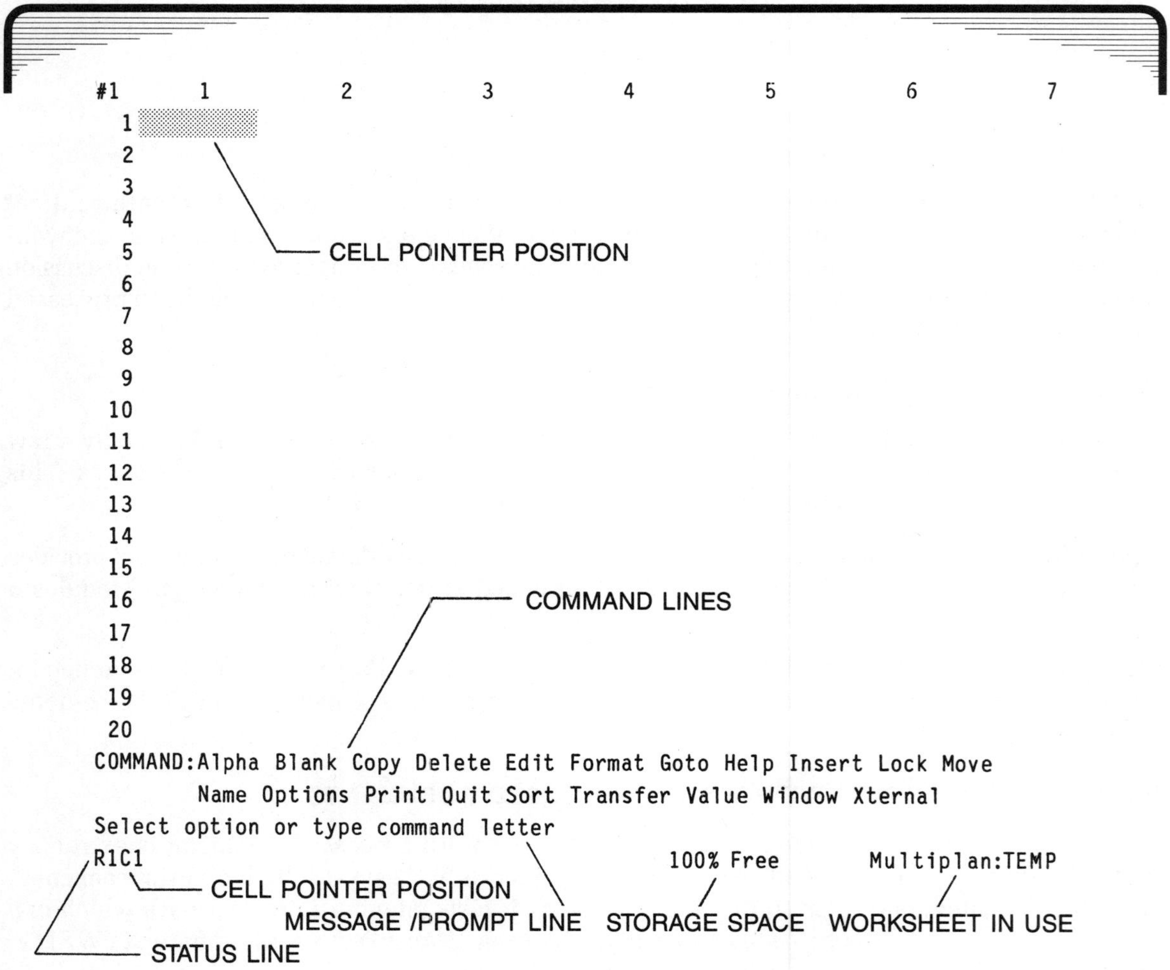

Module 4
RECOMMENDED LEARNING SEQUENCE

INTRODUCTION

This module provides a checklist of module numbers arranged in an order that is recommended for learning Multiplan. The checklist suggests where to start and how to progress through the Multiplan commands. You'll start with simple, easy-to-use, and easy-to-understand commands. As your knowledge of the fundamental Multiplan commands increases, you'll find the advanced commands easier to understand. Within a matter of hours, you'll be using Multiplan to solve real problems of your own.

If you wish, you can study the use and form of Multiplan commands by simply reading the book. However, learning by doing is strongly recommended. There's simply no substitute for actually trying commands on your computer as you read about them. You'll get immediate feedback about their operation, and more importantly, how you can apply them to your own needs.

THE LEARNING SEQUENCE

If you follow the sequence contained in Table 4-1, you'll begin by learning how to use Multiplan's powerful Help utility. Next, a worksheet is built using the Alpha and Value commands. Then you'll learn the rest of Multiplan's commands, beginning with the most frequently used commands and working your way through the commands in a simple-to-complex order. The sequence builds on knowledge. Many of the early commands serve as a basis for more advanced commands, making them easier to understand.

You'll get "sneak previews" of Multiplan commands as you work your way through the early modules. In other words, you'll use new commands in conjunction with ones you're learning so that things work properly. For example, before you learn all the Transfer commands, the Transfer Save and Transfer Load commands are used to save and load files. When new commands are previewed, they are also explained so that you'll understand their purpose. If you're curious about some of these new commands, you may want to find out more about them by turning to the appropriate Module.

When you finish this book, you'll be a competent worksheet programmer. You should be comfortable with the design and use worksheets of all kinds, because you'll have created, formatted, edited, printed, filed, and retrieved a number of different kinds of worksheets. You can use these as models for applications of your own. In fact, you may even want to copy some of the practice files, make slight modifications, and then enter and process your own information.

HOW TO GET STARTED

You should recall how you started in the sample session in Module 2. If you don't, turn back to Module 2 and review it. Use a working copy of your Multiplan program in disk drive A. If you have a two-drive system, you may want to save your worksheets on the disk in drive B. To do this, enter *B:* in front of all filenames. If you decide to save your worksheets on the disk in drive A, no drive designator is necessary. Keep an eye on your disk space to ensure that you don't exceed its capacity.

Table 4-1 Recommended Learning Sequence Checklist

Sequence		Command(s)	Module	Page
□	1	HELP	12	63
□	2	ALPHA	5	27
□	3	VALUE	24	127
□	4	QUIT	21	109
□	5	BLANK	6	33
□	6	EDIT	9	47
□	7	COPY	7	37
□	8	INSERT	13	67
□	9	MOVE	17	89
□	10	DELETE	8	43
□	11	FORMAT	10	51
□	12	PRINT	20	103
□	13	NAME	18	93
□	14	GOTO	11	59
□	15	SORT	22	111
□	16	LOCK	14	71
□	17	OPTIONS	19	97
□	18	TRANSFER	23	117
□	19	WINDOW	25	135
□	20	EXTERNAL	26	143
□	21	MACROS	16	79
□	22	LOOKUP	15	75

Module 5

ALPHA

DESCRIPTION

The Alpha command is used to enter text into a worksheet cell. By definition, text includes alphabetical or numerical characters, punctuation marks, or symbols. Alpha is the first choice on the command line, and when the worksheet is displayed, the Alpha command is highlighted, which means it's ready for use.

THE "OOPS" KEY Before getting into Alpha, there's an important key that you should know about. If at any time you wish to quit what you're doing and start over, just press the **Esc** key and the command line is redisplayed. You can think of the **Esc** key as the "Oops" key. It's there to let you try again when you make a mistake.

STARTING COMMANDS There are two general ways to activate commands. You can highlight commands by pressing the **Tab** key or **Spacebar** until the command you want to use is highlighted. Then press **Return** to display command selections. The second way to activate a command is to type the first letter of the command name, such as **A** for Alpha; command selections are immediately displayed. This method is usually quicker for most command entries, because you only have to press one key.

STARTING THE ALPHA COMMAND The Alpha command may be started in two ways. First, the cell pointer is positioned to the cell in which you want to enter text. This is done with the cursor keys. Once the cell is highlighted, type **A** for Alpha. The word "ALPHA" appears on the command line, which becomes the entry line. You can type the text of your choice and press **Return** to complete the entry.

The second way to enter text is useful when a series of entries are being made. If you're entering text and numbers and using cursor keys to complete entries without pressing **Return**, typing an alphabetical character starts the Alpha command. Conversely, typing a number or mathematical operator starts the Value command. When a cursor key is used to complete a command, you'll notice "ALPHA/VALUE:" displayed on the entry line. This designates that either an alphabetical letter or a number or sign can be used to start either the Alpha or Value command.

When the Alpha command is started, the following information appears at the bottom of your display screen.

```
ALPHA:

Enter text (no double quotes)
RnCn                                  100% Free     Multiplan: Filename
```

ENTERING TEXT At this point you can type the text of your choice. If you make a typographical error, use the **Back Space** key to back up. If you want to move to the beginning of the text without "rubbing out" the preceding text, use the **F9** key to move the cursor left. Use **F10** to move the cursor right on the text entry line. Once the cursor is positioned, text is automatically inserted. To delete one or more characters, use the **Del** key. Remember, the cursor keys control the cell pointer, not the text entry cursor. Press **Return** once you have entered text and notice that the text appears in the cell.

Some worksheet programs use double quotes to differentiate between text and values. However, double quotes are treated just like any other text character during initial text entry in Multiplan. The only time double quotes are required around text is when the Edit command is used to modify text. This process is described in Module 9.

Also notice that the text within the designated cell appears on the bottom line of the screen. If the text string is longer than ten characters, which is the default cell width, you'll have to reformat the column width to match the length of the longest line of text in that column. The method used to change column widths is described in Module 10.

APPLICATIONS

The Alpha command is one of the most frequently used commands in Multiplan. It is used to enter column and row headings (or labels) and worksheet titles. It can be used to enter vertical and horizontal rules, or when vertical bars, hyphens, underscores, and equal signs are used. These applications are illustrated in the Typical Operation section of this module.

TYPICAL OPERATION

In this illustration the Alpha command is used to enter a worksheet title, column and row headings, and horizontal rules. Begin with the Multiplan diskette in the logged disk drive. If you have a system with two floppy disk drives, the Multiplan program should be on the diskette in drive A. If you have a hard drive, Multiplan should be on drive C or E.

1. Type **MP** and press **Return** to display a blank worksheet.
2. Type **F D C** for Format Default Cells, press **Tab**, press **C** for Cont (Continuous), and press **Return**. This allows text to cross cell boundaries when you are typing long text strings such as titles and notes.
3. Type **F W 20**, for Format Width 20, and press **Return** to set the width of column 1 to 20 characters.
4. Position the cell pointer to R1C2, type **A** for Alpha, type the text shown in the following example, and press **Return**.

```
                 1              2         3         4         5         6
   1                            Product Income and Cost Analysis
```

5. Position the cell pointer to R2C1, type **A** for Alpha, type 20 hyphens (--------------------), and press **Return**. Your worksheet should look like the following illustration.

```
                 1              2         3         4         5         6
   1                            Product Income and Cost Analysis
   2 --------------------
```

6. Type **C R 4**, for Copy Right 4 cells, and press **Return**. This copies the horizontal rule four cells to the right as shown below.

```
                 1              2         3         4         5         6
   1                            Product Income and Cost Analysis
   2 ------------------------------------------------------------
```

7. Using the cursor keys to position the cell pointer and the Alpha command, type the text shown in the following example.

```
                    1                 2         3         4         5         6
 1                            Product Income and Cost Analysis
 2 ----------------------------------------------------------------------
 3 Item                   1 Qtr     2 Qtr     3 Qtr     4 Qtr     Total
 4 ====================
 5 Sales
 6 Labor
 7 Material
 8 Total Cost
 9 ====================       (Use 20 equal signs)
10 Gross Profit Margin
11 Cumulative GPM
12
13 GPM as a % of Sales
14 --------------------       (Use 20 hyphens)
```

8. Copy the horizontal rules on rows 4, 9, and 14 by repeating step 6. The result is shown in the following example.

```
                    1                 2         3         4         5         6
 1                            Product Income and Cost Analysis
 2 ----------------------------------------------------------------------
 3 Item                   1 Qtr     2 Qtr     3 Qtr     4 Qtr     Total
 4 ======================================================================
 5 Sales
 6 Labor
 7 Material
 8 Total Cost
 9 ======================================================================
10 Gross Profit Margin
11 Cumulative GPM
12
13 GPM as a % of Sales
14 ----------------------------------------------------------------------
```

NOTE

In the following step, you'll save your worksheet for later use. If you have a two-drive system, the filename GPM.MP is prefixed with B:. If you have a single drive, omit B: in the next step as well as in later exercises.

9. Save your worksheet for later use by typing **T S**, for Transfer Save, typing the name **B:GPM.MP**, and pressing **Return**.
10. Quit Multiplan by typing **Q** for Quit.

Module 6
BLANK

DESCRIPTION

The Blank command is used to replace the contents of one or more cells with "blanks." The effect is the same as deleting text or values from the specified cell or group of cells. To use the Blank command, simply position the cursor on the cell you want to blank and type **B**. The following display appears.

```
BLANK cells: RnCn

Enter reference to cell or group of cells
RnCn         Cell Contents          99% Free      Multiplan: FILENAME
```

If you're going to blank the named cell, press **Return** and the contents of the current cell are blanked. If you want to blank several cells, you can use the range (:) or union (,) operators to simultaneously blank a series of cells in one operation. This is illustrated in the Typical Operation section of this module.

Something you should know is that formats and names still apply to a cell even after it is blanked. If a blanked cell is referenced in a formula, the value of the cell is interpreted as zero.

To completely eliminate the contents of a cell, you should use the Delete command, described in Module 8.

APPLICATIONS

It's sometimes convenient to use empty cells within a worksheet as a "scratch pad" area to make mathematical calculations. In fact, your worksheet makes a nice desk-top calculator. When you're finished making your calculations, you may want to blank the cells to eliminate clutter from a worksheet before it's saved or printed.

If you create a worksheet by trial and error, you may find that cells you started to use are no longer wanted. When this is the case, the Blank command is used to eliminate unwanted displays.

TYPICAL OPERATION

In this illustration the Blank command is used to eliminate unwanted contents from several cells in one operation. Begin with the Multiplan diskette in the logged disk drive. Then load the GPM.MP worksheet saved in Module 5.

1. Type **MP GPM.MP** and press **Return** to display the GPM.MP worksheet. (If you saved GPM.MP on the diskette in drive B, use B:GPM.MP.) Notice the following display.

```
                  1               2         3         4         5         6
 1                           Product Income and Cost Analysis
 2 ------------------------------------------------------------------------
 3 Item                     1 Qtr     2 Qtr     3 Qtr     4 Qtr     Total
 4 ========================================================================
 5 Sales                      11500     13225  15208.75 17490.063 57423.813
 6 Labor                       5620    6322.5 7112.8125 8001.9141 27057.227
 7 Material                    2445   2811.75 3233.5125 3718.5394 12208.802
 8 Total Cost                  8065   9134.25 10346.325 11720.453 39266.028
 9 ========================================================================
10 Gross Profit Margin         3435   4090.75  4862.425 5769.6091 18157.784
11 Cumulative GPM              3435   7525.75 12388.175 18157.784
12
13 GPM as a % of Sales 0.2986957 0.3093195 0.3197123 0.3298793 0.3162065
14 ------------------------------------------------------------------------
```

2. Blank the cells in row 5 beginning with column 2 and ending with column 5; at the same time, blank the contents of cell R6C2 as follows:
   a. Position the cell pointer to R5C2.
   b. Enter the following keystrokes:

Keystrokes	*Results*
B	BLANK cells: R5C2
:	BLANK cells: R5C2:
Right Arrow to R5C5	BLANK cells: R5C2:RC[+3]
,	BLANK cells: R5C2:RC[+3],
Down Arrow to R6C2	BLANK cells: R5C2:RC[+3],R[+1]C
Return	Completes Blank command

3. Notice that the specified cells are blanked, and the values that depend on the blanked cells are either changed or contain an error message.

```
                    1              2          3          4          5          6
 1                        Product Income and Cost Analysis
 2 ----------------------------------------------------------------------
 3 Item                    1 Qtr      2 Qtr      3 Qtr      4 Qtr      Total
 4 ======================================================================
 5 Sales                                                                   0
 6 Labor                                      0          0          0          0
 7 Material                     2445    2811.75 3233.5125 3718.5394 12208.802
 8 Total Cost                   2445    2811.75 3233.5125 3718.5394 12208.802
 9 ======================================================================
10 Gross Profit Margin         -2445   -2811.75 -3233.513 -3718.539   -12208.8
11 Cumulative GPM              -2445   -5256.75 -8490.263  -12208.8
12
13 GPM as a % of Sales   #DIV/0!    #DIV/0!    #DIV/0!    #DIV/0!    #DIV/0!
14 ----------------------------------------------------------------------
```

NOTE

The GPM.MP worksheet is used again; to avoid overwriting it, quit without saving by performing the following step.

4. Quit without saving by typing **Q N**; the operating system prompt is displayed.

Module 7
COPY

DESCRIPTION

The Copy command is used to copy the contents of one or more cells into one or more other cells. The command duplicates text, numbers, or formulas. There are two general forms of the Copy command. First, you can copy the contents of one or more cells beginning with the current cell down or right to one or more designated cells. Second, you can copy from one or more designated cells into the current cell or into a series of cells beginning with the current cell. The *current cell* is the highlighted cell, or the cell designated by the cell pointer. All forms of the Copy command are described in this module.

If you wish to follow along on your computer, you may. The Copy command is started by typing **C**; the following display appears at the bottom of your screen.

```
COPY: Right Down From

Select option or type command letter
RnCn          Cell Contents            99% Free      Multiplan: FILENAME
```

Typing **R** starts the Copy Right command, typing **D** starts the Copy Down command, and typing **F** starts the Copy From command. Each of these forms is explained in this section.

COPY RIGHT The Copy Right command copies one or more cells in a column to the right a specified number of columns. The command form is

```
COPY RIGHT number of cells:        starting at: RnCn

Enter a number
RnCn          Cell Contents            99% Free      Multiplan: FILENAME
```

For example, if you want to copy the contents of cell R3C4 right one cell, position the cell pointer to R3C4 and type

Keystrokes	*Results*
C R	COPY RIGHT number of cells:
1	number of cells: 1
Return	Completes Copy command

If you want to copy the contents of several cells in a column—for instances cells R3C4 through R5C4—into the cells three columns to the right, position the cell pointer to R3C4 and type

Keystrokes	*Results*
C R	COPY RIGHT number of cells:
3	number of cells: 3
Tab	starting at: R3C4
:	starting at: R3C4:
Down Arrow to R5C4	starting at: R3C4:R5C4
Return	Completes Copy command

The contents of R3C4 through R5C4 are copied to rows 3 through 5 of columns 5 through 7.

COPY DOWN The Copy Down command copies one or more cells in a row downward a specified number of rows. The command form is

```
COPY DOWN number of cells:        starting at: RnCn

Enter a number
RnCn         Cell Contents         99% Free     Multiplan: FILENAME
```

For example, if you want to copy the contents of cell R3C4 down one cell, position the cell pointer to R3C4 and type

Keystrokes	*Results*
C D	COPY DOWN number of cells:
1	number of cells: 1
Return	Completes Copy

If you want to copy the contents of several cells in a row—for instance, cells R3C4 through R3C6—into the cells three rows below, position the cell pointer to R3C4 and type

Keystrokes	*Results*
C D	COPY DOWN number of cells:
3	number of cells: 3
Tab	starting at: R3C4
:	starting at: R3C4:
Right Arrow to R3C6	starting at: R3C4:R3C6
Return	Completes Copy

The contents of R3C4 through R3C6 are copied to rows 4 through 6 of columns 4 through 6.

COPY FROM The Copy From command lets you copy the contents of a single cell, a column of cells, a row of cells, or a square or rectangular area of cells. The designated cells or areas of cells are copied beginning at the cell pointer position. If the From cells form a square or rectangular area, the cell marked by the cell pointer is the upper-left-hand corner of the copied area. The command form for Copy From is

```
COPY FROM cells: RnCn          to cells: RnCn

Enter reference to cell or group of cells
RnCn        Cell Contents          99% Free     Multiplan: FILENAME
```

For example, if you want to copy the contents of cell R3C4 into cell R5C3, position the cell pointer to R5C3 and type

Keystrokes	*Results*
C F	COPY FROM cells: R5C3
Cell pointer to R3C4	COPY FROM cells: R3C4
Return	Completes Copy

Assume that you want to copy the contents of a rectangular area of cells into another part of your worksheet, beginning with R9C2 as the upper-left-hand corner. The From area starts with R2C2 in the upper-left-hand corner and R5C6 at the bottom-right-hand corner. To copy the cell area, position the cell pointer to R9C2 (which becomes the upper-left cell of the To area) and type

Keystrokes	*Results*
C F	COPY FROM cells: R9C2
Cell Pointer to R2C2	COPY FROM cells: R2C2
:	COPY FROM cells: R2C2:
Cell Pointer to R5C6	COPY FROM cells: R2C2:R5C6
Return	Completes Copy

The contents of R2C2 through R5C6 are copied to rows 9 through 12 of columns 2 through 6.

You can also use the union operator (,) with the Copy From command. For example, if you want to copy two cell areas, a cell area and a single cell, or several disconnected cells, the command lines might read

COPY FROM cells: R2C2:R5C6,R7C3:R7C5 to cells: R9C2

COPY FROM cells: R2C2,R3C3,R4C4 to cells: R9C2,R15C2

The second example copies the From cells into two different areas of the worksheet, where R9C2 is the upper-left cell of the first area and R15C2 is the upper-left cell of the second area. As you can see, the Copy From command is quite flexible.

APPLICATIONS

The Copy command saves a great deal of time when formulas, rules, or entire tables are needed in two or more areas of a worksheet. It eliminates the need to retype cell entries; in addition, it copies information verbatim, reducing the potential for typographical errors.

You can also use the Copy command to reproduce long formulas or text strings that require only minor changes. Once they have been copied, you can use the Edit command (Module 9) to make changes; this eliminates the need to reconstruct the formulas or text strings from scratch.

TYPICAL OPERATION

In this illustration the Copy command is used to copy an entire worksheet area into another portion of the worksheet. Begin with Multiplan in the logged disk drive. Start by loading the GPM.MP worksheet saved in Module 5.

1. Type **MP GPM.MP** and press **Return** to display the GPM.MP worksheet. (If you saved GPM.MP on the diskette in drive B, use the B:GPM.MP.) Notice the following display.

```
                      1           2         3         4         5         6
 1                          Product Income and Cost Analysis
 2 ----------------------------------------------------------------------
 3 Item                 1 Qtr     2 Qtr     3 Qtr     4 Qtr     Total
 4 ======================================================================
 5 Sales                    11500     13225  15208.75 17490.063 57423.813
 6 Labor                     5620    6322.5 7112.8125 8001.9141 27057.227
 7 Material                  2445   2811.75 3233.5125 3718.5394 12208.802
 8 Total Cost                8065   9134.25 10346.325 11720.453 39266.028
 9 ======================================================================
10 Gross Profit Margin       3435   4090.75  4862.425 5769.6091 18157.784
11 Cumulative GPM            3435   7525.75 12388.175 18157.784
12
13 GPM as a % of Sales 0.2986957 0.3093195 0.3197123 0.3298793 0.3162065
14 ----------------------------------------------------------------------
```

2. Copy the entire worksheet area beginning at R1C1 and ending with R14C6 to another area of the same worksheet starting at cell R16C1 as follows:

   a. Position the cell pointer to R16C1.

b. Enter the following keystrokes:

Keystrokes	*Results*
C F	COPY FROM cells: R16C1
Cell Pointer to R1C1	COPY FROM cells: R1C1
:	COPY FROM cells: R1C1:
Cell Pointer to R14C6	COPY FROM cells: R1C1:R14C6
Return	Completes Copy From command

3. Notice that the specified worksheet area is copied; the upper-left-hand cell of the copied area is R16C1.

```
                   1           2         3         4         5         6
 1                        Product Income and Cost Analysis
 2 ----------------------------------------------------------------------
 3 Item                    1 Qtr     2 Qtr     3 Qtr     4 Qtr     Total
 4 ======================================================================
 5 Sales                   11500      13225  15208.75 17490.063 57423.813
 6 Labor                    5620     6322.5 7112.8125 8001.9141 27057.227
 7 Material                 2445    2811.75 3233.5125 3718.5394 12208.802
 8 Total Cost               8065    9134.25 10346.325 11720.453 39266.028
 9 ======================================================================
10 Gross Profit Margin      3435    4090.75  4862.425 5769.6091 18157.784
11 Cumulative GPM           3435    7525.75 12388.175 18157.784
12
13 GPM as a % of Sales 0.2986957 0.3093195 0.3197123 0.3298793 0.3162065
14 ----------------------------------------------------------------------
15
16                        Product Income and Cost Analysis
17 ----------------------------------------------------------------------
18 Item                    1 Qtr     2 Qtr     3 Qtr     4 Qtr     Total
19 ======================================================================
20 Sales                   11500      13225  15208.75 17490.063 57423.813
21 Labor                    5620     6322.5 7112.8125 8001.9141 27057.227
22 Material                 2445    2811.75 3233.5125 3718.5394 12208.802
23 Total Cost               8065    9134.25 10346.325 11720.453 39266.028
24 ======================================================================
25 Gross Profit Margin      3435    4090.75  4862.425 5769.6091 18157.784
26 Cumulative GPM           3435    7525.75 12388.175 18157.784
27
28 GPM as a % of Sales 0.2986957 0.3093195 0.3197123 0.3298793 0.3162065
29 ----------------------------------------------------------------------
```

4. To prevent overwriting the GPM.MP worksheet, which will be used again, quit without saving by typing **Q N**; the operating system prompt is displayed.

Module 8

DELETE

DESCRIPTION

The Delete command is used to delete (or erase) one or more entire rows or columns or a continuous series of cells in one or more rows or columns within a worksheet. The form for the Delete command is

```
DELETE: Row Column

Select option or type command letter
RnCn        Cell Contents          99% Free     Multiplan: FILENAME
```

The following two paragraphs describe the Delete Row and Delete Column commands.

DELETE ROW Two examples of the Delete Row command are described. The first deletes a single row, while the second deletes a series of cells within three rows.

To delete row 3 of a worksheet, position the cell pointer to row 3 and type

Keystroke	*Results*	
D R	DELETE ROW # of rows: 1	starting at row: 3
Return	Completes Delete Row command.	

To delete a series of cells between columns 2 and 5 in rows 3 and 4, position the cell pointer to R3C2 and type

Keystroke	*Results*	
D R	DELETE ROW # of rows: 1	starting at row: 3
2	DELETE ROW # of rows: 2	before row: 3
Tab Tab	between columns: 1	and: 255
2 Tab	between columns: 2	and: 255
5	between columns: 2	and: 5
Return	Completes Insert Row command.	

DELETE COLUMN Two examples of the Delete Column command are also described. The first deletes a single column, while the second deletes a series of cells within a column.

To delete column 3 of a worksheet, position the cell pointer to column 3 and type

Keystroke	*Results*	
D C	DELETE COLUMN # of columns: 1	starting at: 3
Return	Completes Delete Column command.	

To delete a series of cells between rows 2 and 5 in columns 3 and 4, position the cell pointer to R2C3 and type

Keystroke	*Results*	
D C	DELETE COLUMN # of columns: 1	starting at: 3
2	DELETE COLUMN # of columns: 2	starting at: 3
Tab Tab	between rows: 1	and: 4095
2 Tab	between rows: 2	and: 4095
5	between rows: 2	and: 5
Return	Completes Insert Column command.	

When relative values are used, Multiplan adds the rows or columns necessary to maintain formula integrity. However, if you use absolute cell addresses, the Delete command should be used sparingly, as you may be required to edit cell references within your formulas. If cell names are used, as described in Module 18, the Delete command won't affect cell references in formulas that use names for cell references.

APPLICATIONS

You can use the Delete command to eliminate unwanted rows, columns, or cell areas from your worksheet. You can also use it to "pull" rows, columns, or cell areas up or to the left on your worksheet by eliminating blank or unwanted areas. This helps you attain the desired worksheet appearance.

The Delete command completely eliminates the contents of the specified cell or cells. This action "deallocates" the deleted cell or cells from your computer's memory. In contrast, the Blank command (see Module 6) replaces contents with blank spaces. Format and name attributes are also eliminated when one or more cells are deleted.

TYPICAL OPERATION

In this illustration the Delete command is used to delete row 12 from the GPM.MP worksheet. Begin with Multiplan diskette in the logged disk drive, and load the GPM.MP worksheet saved in Module 5.

1. Type **MP GPM.MP** and press **Return** to display the GPM.MP worksheet. (If you saved GPM.MP on the diskette in drive B, use B:GMP.MP.) Notice the following display.

```
                 1             2         3         4         5         6
 1                    Product Income and Cost Analysis
 2 ----------------------------------------------------------------------
 3 Item                   1 Qtr     2 Qtr     3 Qtr     4 Qtr     Total
 4 ======================================================================
 5 Sales                      11500     13225  15208.75 17490.063 57423.813
 6 Labor                       5620    6322.5 7112.8125 8001.9141 27057.227
 7 Material                    2445   2811.75 3233.5125 3718.5394 12208.802
 8 Total Cost                  8065   9134.25 10346.325 11720.453 39266.028
 9 ======================================================================
10 Gross Profit Margin         3435   4090.75  4862.425 5769.6091 18157.784
11 Cumulative GPM              3435   7525.75 12388.175 18157.784
12
13 GPM as a % of Sales 0.2986957 0.3093195 0.3197123 0.3298793 0.3162065
14 ----------------------------------------------------------------------
```

2. Position the cell pointer to row 12 and type

Keystroke	*Results*
D R	DELETE ROW # of rows: 1 starting at row: 12
Return	Completes Delete Row command.

3. Notice that the blank row that previously occupied the row 12 position is deleted; former row 13 is now row 12.

```
                 1             2         3         4         5         6
 1                    Product Income and Cost Analysis
 2 ----------------------------------------------------------------------
 3 Item                   1 Qtr     2 Qtr     3 Qtr     4 Qtr     Total
 4 ======================================================================
 5 Sales                      11500     13225  15208.75 17490.063 57423.813
 6 Labor                       5620    6322.5 7112.8125 8001.9141 27057.227
 7 Material                    2445   2811.75 3233.5125 3718.5394 12208.802
 8 Total Cost                  8065   9134.25 10346.325 11720.453 39266.028
 9 ======================================================================
10 Gross Profit Margin         3435   4090.75  4862.425 5769.6091 18157.784
11 Cumulative GPM              3435   7525.75 12388.175 18157.784
12 GPM as a % of Sales 0.2986957 0.3093195 0.3197123 0.3298793 0.3162065
13 ----------------------------------------------------------------------
```

4. To prevent overwriting the GPM.MP worksheet, which will be used again, quit without saving by typing **Q N**; the operating system prompt is displayed.

Module 9

EDIT

DESCRIPTION

The Edit command is used to change the contents of a cell. You can change text, numbers, or formulas with this command. It is used by moving the cell pointer to the cell to be changed and typing **E** for Edit. The following display appears at the bottom of the screen.

```
EDIT : "Cell Contents"_

Enter a formula
RnCn        Cell Contents            99% Free     Multiplan: FILENAME
```

Remember, the cursor control keys are used to position the cell pointer, not the cursor on the data entry line. This cursor is controlled as follows:

Function	***Key Sequence***
Char Left	F9 or Ctrl-K
Char Right	F10 or Ctrl-L
Word Left	F7 or Ctrl-O
Word Right	F8 or Ctrl-P
Back Space (Rubout)	Back Space or Ctrl-H
Delete	Del

Cells containing Alpha entries begin and end with double quotes. Before you can leave the Edit session, you must surround your Alpha entries with double quotes. Cells containing Value entries do not require (or display) quotes.

APPLICATIONS

The Edit command is used to make minor changes to text or values within a selected cell. The alternative to using the Edit command is to position the cell pointer to the cell to be changed and then retype the entire entry using the Alpha or Value command. This is time consuming when the entry is lengthy, or contains a complex formula. Therefore, the Edit command is recommended as the most efficient way to modify cell contents.

TYPICAL OPERATION

In this illustration the Edit command is used to change the title of an existing worksheet. Begin with Multiplan in the logged disk drive, and load the GPM.MP worksheet saved in Module 5.

1. Type **MP GPM.MP** and press **Return** to display the GPM.MP worksheet. (If you saved GPM.MP on the diskette in drive B, use B:GPM.MP.) Notice the following display.

```
                 1            2          3          4          5          6
 1                     Product Income and Cost Analysis
 2 ----------------------------------------------------------------------
 3 Item                 1 Qtr      2 Qtr      3 Qtr      4 Qtr      Total
 4 ======================================================================
 5 Sales                  11500      13225   15208.75  17490.063  57423.813
 6 Labor                   5620     6322.5  7112.8125  8001.9141  27057.227
 7 Material                2445    2811.75  3233.5125  3718.5394  12208.802
 8 Total Cost              8065    9134.25  10346.325  11720.453  39266.028
 9 ======================================================================
10 Gross Profit Margin     3435    4090.75   4862.425  5769.6091  18157.784
11 Cumulative GPM          3435    7525.75  12388.175  18157.784
12
13 GPM as a % of Sales 0.2986957 0.3093195 0.3197123 0.3298793 0.3162065
14 ----------------------------------------------------------------------
```

2. Position the cell pointer to R1C2 and press **E** to edit the title. Notice the following text on the data entry line.

```
EDIT : "Product Income and Cost Analysis"

Enter a formula
R1C2     "Product Income and Cost A    99% Free     Multiplan: GPM.MP
```

3. Using the Char Left, Char Right, and **Del** keys, change the title to read

```
EDIT : "Revenue and Expense Analysis"

Enter a formula
R1C2     "Product Income and Cost A   99% Free    Multiplan: GPM.MP
```

4. Press **Return** and notice that the title has been changed as shown in the following illustration.

```
              1             2         3         4         5         6
1                      Revenue and Expense Analysis
2 ----------------------------------------------------------------------
3 Item                 1 Qtr     2 Qtr     3 Qtr     4 Qtr     Total
4 ======================================================================
5 Sales                    11500     13225  15208.75 17490.063 57423.813
```

5. To prevent overwriting the GPM.MP worksheet, which will be used again, quit without saving by typing **Q N**; the operating system prompt is displayed.

Module 10

FORMAT

DESCRIPTION

The Format command is used to control the way numbers are displayed, to adjust the width of one or more columns, and to change Multiplan format default values. The form for the Format command is

```
FORMAT: Cells Default Options Width

Select option or type command letter
RnCn        Cell Contents          99% Free     Multiplan: FILENAME
```

The following four paragraphs describe the Cells, Default, Options, and Width selections.

FORMAT CELLS Typing **F C** displays the Format Cells options. This display looks like the following example:

```
FORMAT cells: RnCn                alignment: (Def)Ctr Gen Left Right -
      format code: (Def)Cont Exp Fix Gen Int $ * % -     # of decimals: 0
Enter reference to cell or group of cells
RnCn        Cell Contents          99% Free     Multiplan: FILENAME
```

The Format Cells command gives you four selections. These are:

- cells: RnCn
- alignment: (Def) Ctr Gen Left Right -
- format code: (Def) Cont Exp Fix Gen Int $ * % -
- # of decimals: 0

You can move between selections with the **Tab** key. Pressing the first letter of a choice, such as **C** for "Ctr" or **F** for "Fix," assigns these format values to the cell or range of cells entered following the "cells:" selection. Notice that default selections are surrounded with parentheses. The parentheses shift according to your selection. Each selection area is explained below, and an example is given to show you how to maneuver within the Format Cells command.

cells: Here, the cell at which the cell pointer is located is displayed. You can use the **Back Space** key and retype any cell or range of cells of your choosing. If you want to assign format control to all cells in a rectangular area with R2C3 at the upper left and R12C10 at the lower right, you can use the range operator (:) by typing

R2C3:R12C10 or R2:12C3:10

You can also use the union operator (,) to specify individual cells or multiple ranges. Once you've selected the cells, press the **Tab** key to move to the alignment selection.

alignment: Alignment lets you position text within the specified cells. The default (Def) alignment uses Multiplan's general (Gen) format alignment, which adjusts text flush left and numbers flush right. The Gen format also displays numbers as precisely as possible and automatically uses scientific notation as needed. If the Format Default command is used to change from general alignment, the alignment values established by the Format Default command are used. Format Default is explained in the next major paragraph of this section.

Typing **C**, **L**, or **R** positions text and numbers center, flush left, or flush right. Typing **D** returns alignment to default. Typing **-** leaves the alignment selection unchanged and moves the cursor to the format code selection area.

format code: There are several format codes to choose from. They are summarized in the following list.

Cont	Allows text to be typed continuously, crossing cell boundaries as necessary. Typically used for worksheet titles and notes.
Def	Uses default format, which is normally Gen, but which can be adjusted by the Format Default command.
Exp	Displays numbers in scientific notation (powers of ten).
Fix	Works with "# of decimals" selection to fix the number of decimal places displayed.
Gen	Displays numbers as precisely as possible; uses scientific notation automatically when required.
Int	Displays decimal fractions as integers (whole numbers).
$	Displays numbers as dollars and cents.

*	Displays numbers as a row of asterisks for bar graph presentation. If a number exceeds the available spaces within a row, it may be necessary to widen the cell using the Format Width command.
%	Works with the "# of decimals" selection to display numbers as a percentage. For example, .5 is displayed as 50% if # of decimals = 0. The display is 50.00% if # of decimals = 2.

# of decimals: This selection works in conjunction with the Fix and % format codes. When Fix or % is selected, press the **Tab** key to advance to the "# of decimals" selection. Then type a number to fix the number of decimal places displayed in the specified cells.

Multiplan also features several formatting operators used within formulas to do such things as fixing decimal places or displaying dollars and cents. These operators are described in Appendix E. Because you can achieve the same results with formatting operators as with the Format command, there may be cases where a formatting operator is preferable. For example, if you have a formula that you plan to copy several times, you may want to include an embedded formatting operator so that format is automatically controlled within the expression.

Example To illustrate the use of the Format Cells command, assume that you want to center column headings in columns 2 through 5 of row 3, and to display numbers in columns 2 through 5 of rows 5 through 8 as dollars and cents. To center the column headings, position the cell pointer to cell R3C2 and type

Keystroke	*Results*
F C	FORMAT cells: R3C2
:	FORMAT cells: R3C2:
Cell Pointer to R3C5	FORMAT cells: R3C2:R3C5
Tab	alignment: (Def)Ctr Gen Left Right -
C	alignment: Def(Ctr)Gen Left Right -
Return	Completes Format Cells command.

To display the numbers in columns 2 through 5 of rows 5 through 8 as dollars and cents, position the cell pointer to R5C2 and type

Keystroke	*Results*
F C	FORMAT cells: R5C2
:	FORMAT cells: R5C2:
Cell Pointer to R8C5	FORMAT cells: R3C2:R8C5
Tab	alignment: (Def)Ctr Gen Left Right -
Tab	format code: (Def)Cont Exp Fix Gen Int $ * % -
$	format code: Def Cont Exp Fix Gen Int($)* % -
Return	Completes Format Cells command.

FORMAT DEFAULT The Format Default command is used to assign format control to all cells that are not otherwise formatted with the Format Cells or Format Width commands. As a rule, you should determine the format for the majority of worksheet cells and establish it before you begin entering data. This should minimize the amount of formatting work required during worksheet preparation. When you type **F D** the following selections are displayed.

```
FORMAT DEFAULT: Cells Width

Select option or type command letter
RnCn        Cell Contents          99% Free     Multiplan: FILENAME
```

Format Default Cells The Format Default Cells command lets you establish alignment, format code, and # of decimals format controls. Typing **C** displays the following selections.

```
FORMAT DEFAULT CELLS alignment: Ctr Gen Left Right
       format code: Cont Exp Fix(Gen)Int $ * %    # of decimals: 0
Select option
RnCn        Cell Contents          99% Free     Multiplan: FILENAME
```

Notice that the established default is General, which positions text flush left, and numbers flush right, and which displays numbers as precisely as possible. If a number exceeds the width of a cell, scientific notation is used.

The "alignment," "format," and "# of decimals" selections are explained in the FORMAT CELLS paragraph of this section.

Format Default Width The Format Default Width command lets you establish a default width. The default normally used is ten characters. However, if you wish to change the default width, type **F D W** from the command line; the following selections are displayed.

```
FORMAT DEFAULT width in chars: 10

Enter a number
RnCn        Cell Contents          99% Free     Multiplan: FILENAME
```

At this point you can change the Default Width value by typing the number of your choice between 3 and 32.

FORMAT OPTIONS The Format Options command is used to display numbers with commas or to display formulas instead of resulting formula values. The Format Options display is created by typing **F O**; the following selections are displayed.

```
FORMAT OPTIONS commas: Yes No        formulas: Yes(No)

Select option
RnCn        Cell Contents          99% Free     Multiplan: FILENAME
```

Format Options Commas The Format Options commas command is used to display commas in numbers having four digits or more. When using this option, you should ensure that your cell widths are large enough to accommodate the increased character spaces occupied by the commas. To select comma display, simply type **Y** and press **Return**.

Format Options Formulas The Format Options formulas command displays formulas instead of the derived numerical or logical values. To use this selection, simply press the **Tab** key. You can use the formulas selection to "debug" a worksheet by displaying formulas so that they can be visually checked.

FORMAT WIDTH The Format Width command is used to change the width of one or more columns of the active worksheet. Typing **F W** displays the following selections.

```
FORMAT WIDTH in chars or d(efault): d     column: 1     through: 1

Enter a number, or d for default
RnCn        Cell Contents          99% Free     Multiplan: FILENAME
```

Typing **d** results in the Format Width default value, which is 10 unless it is specifically changed by using the Format Width default command. Pressing the **Tab** key moves the cursor to other selections on the data entry line. You may type the beginning column number after the "column:" selection. If you want to change the width of more than one cell, **Tab** to the "through:" selection and enter the ending column number.

APPLICATIONS

The Format commands are used to display worksheet information exactly as you want it to appear. You can display numbers as dollar values, as percentages, with commas, or even as horizontal bar graphs. You can fix decimal values to a specified number of places. You can position text and values either center, left, or right within cells. You can change the width of cells to see a larger portion of your worksheet, to make it fit on a single sheet of paper when printed, or to allow a large number to fit within a cell. And you can display formulas instead of values, to help you check their accuracy. All of these features make the Format command an extremely useful tool.

TYPICAL OPERATION

In this illustration you use the Format command to center column headings and to display numbers as dollar and percentage values. Begin with Multiplan in the logged disk drive, and load the GPM.MP worksheet saved in Module 5.

1. Type **MP GPM.MP** and press **Return** to display the GPM.MP worksheet. (If you saved GPM.MP on the diskette in drive B, use B:GPM.MP.) Notice the following display.

```
                  1              2          3          4          5          6
 1                         Product Income and Cost Analysis
 2 ----------------------------------------------------------------------
 3 Item                   1 Qtr      2 Qtr      3 Qtr      4 Qtr      Total
 4 ======================================================================
 5 Sales                    11500      13225   15208.75  17490.063  57423.813
 6 Labor                     5620     6322.5  7112.8125  8001.9141  27057.227
 7 Material                  2445    2811.75  3233.5125  3718.5394  12208.802
 8 Total Cost                8065    9134.25  10346.325  11720.453  39266.028
 9 ======================================================================
10 Gross Profit Margin       3435    4090.75   4862.425  5769.6091  18157.784
11 Cumulative GPM            3435    7525.75  12388.175  18157.784
12
13 GPM as a % of Sales 0.2986957 0.3093195 0.3197123 0.3298793 0.3162065
14 ----------------------------------------------------------------------
```

2. Center the headings of columns 2 through 6 by positioning the cell pointer to R3C2 and typing

Keystroke	*Results*
F C	FORMAT cells: R3C2
:	FORMAT cells: R3C2:
Cell Pointer to R3C6	FORMAT cells: R3C2:R3C6
Tab	alignment: (Def)Ctr Gen Left Right -
C	alignment: Def(Ctr)Gen Left Right -
Return	Completes Format Cells command.

3. Display the values in columns 2 through 6 of rows 5 through 11 as dollars and cents by positioning the cell pointer to R5C2 and typing

Keystroke	*Results*
F C	FORMAT cells: R5C2
:	FORMAT cells: R5C2:
Cell Pointer to R11C6	FORMAT cells: R3C2:R11C6
Tab	alignment: (Def)Ctr Gen Left Right -
Tab	format code: (Def)Cont Exp Fix Gen Int $ * % -
$	format code: Def Cont Exp Fix Gen Int($)* % -
Return	Completes Format Cells command.

4. Display the values in columns 2 through 6 of row 13 as a percentage to two decimal places by positioning the cell pointer to R13C2 and typing

Keystroke	*Results*
F C	FORMAT cells: R13C2
:	FORMAT cells: R13C2:
Cell Pointer to R13C6	FORMAT cells: R13C2:R13C6
Tab	alignment: (Def)Ctr Gen Left Right -
Tab	format code: (Def)Cont Exp Fix Gen Int $ * % -
%	format code: Def Cont Exp Fix Gen Int $ *(%)-
Tab	# of decimals: 0
2	# of decimals: 2
Return	Completes Format Cells command.

5. Notice that the worksheet looks like the following illustration.

```
                  1              2         3         4         5         6
 1                        Product Income and Cost Analysis
 2 ------------------------------------------------------------------------
 3 Item                    1 Qtr     2 Qtr     3 Qtr     4 Qtr     Total
 4 ========================================================================
 5 Sales              $11500.00 $13225.00 $15208.75 $17490.06 $57423.81
 6 Labor               $5620.00  $6322.50  $7112.81  $8001.91 $27057.23
 7 Material            $2445.00  $2811.75  $3233.51  $3718.54 $12208.80
 8 Total Cost          $8065.00  $9134.25 $10346.33 $11720.45 $39266.03
 9 ========================================================================
10 Gross Profit Margin $3435.00  $4090.75  $4862.43  $5769.61 $18157.78
11 Cumulative GPM      $3435.00  $7525.75 $12388.18 $18157.78
12
13 GPM as a % of Sales      29.87%    30.93%    31.97%    32.99%    31.62%
14 ------------------------------------------------------------------------
```

6. Save the formatted worksheet by typing **T S Y**, for Transfer Save Yes.
7. Quit by typing **Q** for Quit; the operating system prompt is displayed.

Module 11
GOTO

DESCRIPTION

The Goto command is used to move the cell pointer to a desired cell or to a worksheet window. The pointer is moved to the desired cell by specifying a row-column position or a cell name. Window command is described in Module 25. If the "goto" cell is presently displayed, the cell pointer jumps to it. If the "goto" cell is on part of the worksheet that is off-screen, the worksheet area containing the cell is brought into view along with the specified cell.

The form of the Goto command is

```
GOTO: Macro Name Row-col Window

Select option or type command letter
RnCn         Cell Contents          99% Free      Multiplan: FILENAME
```

Some examples of the Goto command are contained in the following paragraphs of this section to illustrate its use.

GOTO MACRO The Macro option is used to run a macro (see Module 16). To run a macro, you must enter the cell reference or the macro name. If you don't remember the macro names, you can display the names automatically with the left and right cursor keys. The form of the command is

```
GOTO macro:

Enter reference to cell or group of cells
RnCn         Cell Contents          99% Free      Multiplan: FILENAME
```

GOTO NAME The Goto Name command is used to jump the cell pointer to the cell having the specified name. The form of this command is

```
GOTO name:

Enter reference to cell or group of cells
RnCn        Cell Contents          99% Free     Multiplan: FILENAME
```

To jump the cell pointer to a cell having the name "Subtotal," type

Keystrokes	*Results*
G	GOTO: Name Row-col Window
N	GOTO name:
Subtotal	GOTO name: Subtotal
Return	Completes Goto Name command

GOTO ROW-COL The Goto Row-col command is used to jump the cell pointer to a cell by specifying the absolute row-column reference. The form of this command is

```
GOTO row:          column:

Enter a number
RnCn        Cell Contents          99% Free     Multiplan: FILENAME
```

To jump the cell pointer to cell R25C8, type

Keystrokes	*Results*	
G	GOTO: Name Row-col Window	
R	GOTO row: 1	column: 1
25	GOTO row: 25	column: 1
Tab 8	GOTO row: 25	column: 8
Return	Completes Goto Row-Col	command

GOTO WINDOW The Goto Window command is used to jump the cell pointer to a window by specifying the window number. Windows are created with the Window command described in Module 25. The first window is 1, the second 2, and so on. Therefore, if you want to move the cell pointer to window 2, Goto Window 2 does the trick. The Goto Window command also lets you specify a row-column number within a window. The specified row-column is placed at the upper-left-hand corner of the display screen. The window and row-column coordinates at which the cell pointer is located are automatically shown on the data entry line when it is first displayed. The form of this command is

```
GOTO WINDOW window number: n          row: n        column: n

Enter a number
RnCn        Cell Contents          99% Free     Multiplan: FILENAME
```

To jump the cell pointer to row 11 column 6 of window 2, type

Keystrokes	*Results*		
G	GOTO: Name Row-col Window		
W	GOTO WINDOW window number: 1	row: 1	column: 1
2	GOTO WINDOW window number: 2	row: 1	column: 1
Tab 11	GOTO WINDOW window number: 2	row: 11	column:
Tab 6	GOTO WINDOW window number: 2	row: 11	column: 6
Return	Completes Goto Window command		

APPLICATIONS

The Goto command provides a quick way to move to specific cells within a worksheet. The command is especially helpful when cells are named. Using the sequence **G N Total Return** (for Goto Name Total) to jump to the "Total" cell on a large worksheet normally takes less time than moving to the "Total" cell with the cell pointer. This is particularly true if you must scroll several screens to reach the cell. The Goto Window command is required for moving between windows.

TYPICAL OPERATION

In this illustration the Goto command is used to move around in the GPM.MP worksheet created in Module 5, formatted in Module 10, and last saved with named cells in Module 18. Begin with Multiplan in the logged disk drive and the GPM.MP worksheet diskette in drive B.

1. Type **MP GPM.MP** and press **Return** to display the GPM.MP worksheet. (If you saved GPM.MP on the diskette in drive B, use B:GPM.MP.) Notice the following display.

	1	2	3	4	5	6
1		Product Income and Cost Analysis				
2	-------------------	----------	----------	----------	----------	----------
3	Item	1 Qtr	2 Qtr	3 Qtr	4 Qtr	Total
4	===================	==========	==========	==========	==========	==========
5	Sales	$11500.00	$13225.00	$15208.75	$17490.06	$57423.81
6	Labor	$5620.00	$6322.50	$7112.81	$8001.91	$27057.23
7	Material	$2445.00	$2811.75	$3233.51	$3718.54	$12208.80
8	Total Cost	$8065.00	$9134.25	$10346.33	$11720.45	$39266.03
9	===================	==========	==========	==========	==========	==========
10	Gross Profit Margin	$3435.00	$4090.75	$4862.43	$5769.61	$18157.78
11	Cumulative GPM	$3435.00	$7525.75	$12388.18	$18157.78	
12						
13	GPM as a % of Sales	29.87%	30.93%	31.97%	32.99%	31.62%
14	-------------------	----------	----------	----------	----------	----------

2. Move the cell pointer to the beginning of the "Sales" row by typing

Keystrokes	*Results*
G	GOTO: Name Row-col Window
N	GOTO name:
Sales	GOTO name: Sales
Return	Completes Goto Name command

3. Notice that the cell pointer jumps to R5C2, which is the first cell of the "Sales" row.

4. Move the cell pointer to the "Total Cost" cell by typing

Keystrokes	*Results*
G	GOTO: Name Row-col Window
N	GOTO name:
Total_Cost	GOTO name: Total_Cost
Return	Completes Goto Name command

5. Notice that the cell pointer jumps to R8C6, which is the "Total_Cost" cell containing the formula SUM(COST).

6. Move the cell pointer to R13C2 using the Goto Row-col command by typing

Keystrokes	*Results*	
G	GOTO: Name Row-col Window	
R	GOTO row: 8	column: 6
13	GOTO row: 13	column: 6
Tab 2	GOTO row: 13	column: 2
Return	Completes Goto Row-Col	command

7. Quit by typing **Q** for Quit; the operating system prompt is displayed.

Module 12

HELP

DESCRIPTION

The Help command is used to display information about the use of Multiplan commands and operators. General Help information can be displayed by typing **H** from the displayed worksheet. Information about a specific command is displayed by pressing **?** after the command has been started. For example, if you've typed **F** for Format and you want to look up your choices, simply press **?** and the Format Help information is displayed.

```
FORMAT CELLS

Sets a specific format and alignment for one or more cells. Just typing
FC shows the properties of the active cell. Parameters are:

1.  Cell or group of cells to be formatted.
2.  Alignment. Choices are:

Def      Aligns as specified in the format Default command.
Ctr      Centers cell entries
Get      (General) Aligns text left, numbers right.
Left     Aligns cell entries to the left.
Right    Aligns cell entries to the right.
-        Do not change alignment.

3.  Format. Choices are:

Def      Format as specified in the Format Default command.
Cont     Continues long text across column border, if next cell

HELP: Resume Start Next Previous
      Applications Commands Editing Formulas Keyboard Macro
Select option or type command letter
R1C1                                 100% Free      Multiplan: FILENAME
```

Typing **N** for Next displays the next Help screen.

```
          empty and also formatted "Cont".
Exp       (Scientific notation) Displays numbers as a decimal times a
          power of ten. Number of digits as specified in "# of decimals."
Fix       Rounds to and displays number of decimals specified
          in "# of decimals" field.
Gen       (General) Displays numbers in the most appropriate form
          considering the size of the cell and of the number.
Int       Numbers will be shown as integers after rounding.
$         Displays numbers with leading dollar sign and 2 decimal
          places (negative numbers enclosed in parentheses).
*         (Bar Graph) Displays as many asterisks as the value of the number.
%         (percent) Displays the number time 100 followed by a percent sign.
-         Do not change format.

4. Number of decimals. This is used in the Exp, Fix and % formats above.


 FORMAT WIDTH



 HELP: Resume Start Next Previous
       Applications Commands Editing Formulas Keyboard Macro
 Select option or type command letter
 R1C1                                100% Free      Multiplan: FILENAME
```

These two screens of Help information are typical of what is available in Multiplan. Notice your choices at the bottom of the screen. Pressing **R** for Resume, **S** for Start, and so on initiates the Help options. A summary of the choices is given in Table 12-1.

Table 12-1 Help Options

Option	Description
Resume	Returns control to the menu in use or to the command line, depending on where Help was initiated. Pressing ESC also takes you out of the Help mode.
Start	Takes you to the first page of the Help information. Pressing HOME also takes you to the first page.
Next	Shows the next screen of Help information. PAGE DOWN also displays the next screen.
Previous	Shows the previous screen of Help information. PAGE UP also displays the previous screen.
Applications	Lists typical worksheet problems and corresponding commands that offer solutions.
Commands	Displays the beginning screen of command Help information, which is Alpha.
Editing	Displays Help information about worksheet editing.
Formulas	Displays Help information and rules relating to formulas.
Keyboard	Describes the keys used to perform Multiplan functions.
Macro	Displays help information about macro operation and presents a list of macro functions.

APPLICATIONS

Multiplan's on-screen Help information is convenient any time you need to refresh your memory about a particular command, operator, or control key. The real advantage of the Help command is that it lets you zero in on the specific area of need when you need it. The ability to view either general or specific Help information makes this an extremely powerful capability.

TYPICAL OPERATION

In this illustration the Help command is used to review information about the Blank function. Begin with Multiplan in the logged disk drive.

1. Type **MP** and press **Return** to display a blank worksheet.
2. Type **B** for Blank and **?** to display Help information about the Blank command. Notice the following display.

```
The parameter must describe an area of the sheet.  Check if all names
have been defined and also check the use of parentheses and operators.
For more information select "Formulas" (F) on the Help Menu.




HELP: Resume Start Next Previous
      Applications Commands Editing Formulas Keyboard
Select option or type command letter
R1C1                                  100% Free       Multiplan: FILENAME
```

3. Press **Esc** to return to the worksheet command line.
4. Quit Multiplan by typing **Q** for Quit.

Module 13

INSERT

DESCRIPTION

The Insert command is used to insert one or more entire rows or columns or a continuous series of cells in one or more rows or columns within a worksheet. The form for the Insert command is

```
INSERT: Row Column

Select option or type command letter
RnCn          Cell Contents          99% Free     Multiplan: FILENAME
```

The following two paragraphs within this section describe the Insert Row and Insert Column commands.

INSERT ROW Two examples of the Insert Row command are described. The first inserts a single row, while the second inserts a series of cells within a row.

To insert one new row before row 3, position the cell pointer to row 3 and type

Keystroke	*Results*	
I R	INSERT ROW # of rows: 1	before row: 3
Return	Completes Insert Row command.	

To insert a series of cells between columns C2 and C5 in rows 3 and 4, position the cell pointer to R3C2 and type

Keystroke	*Results*	
I R	INSERT ROW # of rows: 1	before row: 3
2	INSERT ROW # of rows: 2	before row: 3
Tab Tab	between columns: 1	and: 255
2 Tab	between columns: 2	and: 255
5	between columns: 2	and: 5
Return	Completes Insert Row command.	

INSERT COLUMN Two examples of the Insert Column command are also described. The first inserts a single column and the second inserts a series of cells within a column.

To insert a new column before column 3, position the cell pointer to column 3 and type

Keystroke	*Results*	
I C	INSERT COLUMN # of columns: 1	before column: 3
Return	Completes Insert Column command.	

To insert a series of cells between rows 2 and 5 in columns 3 and 4, position the cell pointer to R2C3 and type

Keystroke	*Results*	
I C	INSERT COLUMN # of columns: 1	before column: 3
2	INSERT COLUMN # of columns: 2	before column: 3
Tab Tab	between rows: 1	and: 4095
2 Tab	between rows: 2	and: 4095
5	between rows: 2	and: 5
Return	Completes Insert Column command.	

When relative values are used, Multiplan adds the rows or columns necessary to maintain formula integrity. However, with absolute cell addresses, the Insert command should be used sparingly, as you may be required to edit cell references within your formulas. If cell names are used, as described in Module 17, the Insert command won't affect cell references in formulas using names for cell references.

APPLICATIONS

As you design a worksheet, you'll often find that you've overlooked the need for a row, column, or series of cells. This makes the Insert command a lifesaver. You can insert rows or columns as needed to add new data. You may also want to "dress up" your worksheet by adding horizontal or vertical rules. Here again, you can use the Insert command to insert the necessary cells.

You can also use the Insert command to push rows, columns, or cell areas down or to the right on your worksheet to attain the desired alignment.

TYPICAL OPERATION

In this illustration the Insert command is used to add a row between the title of the GPM.MP worksheet and the first horizontal rule. Begin with the Multiplan diskette in the logged disk drive. Then load the GPM.MP worksheet saved in Module 24.

1. Type **MP GPM.MP** and press **Return** to display the GPM.MP worksheet. (If you saved GPM.MP on the diskette in drive B, use B:GPM.MP.) Notice the following display.

```
                 1              2         3         4         5         6
  1                   Product Income and Cost Analysis
  2 ----------------------------------------------------------------------
  3 Item                  1 Qtr     2 Qtr     3 Qtr     4 Qtr     Total
  4 ======================================================================
  5 Sales                     11500     13225  15208.75 17490.063 57423.813
  6 Labor                      5620    6322.5 7112.8125 8001.9141 27057.227
  7 Material                   2445   2811.75 3233.5125 3718.5394 12208.802
  8 Total Cost                 8065   9134.25 10346.325 11720.453 39266.028
  9 ======================================================================
 10 Gross Profit Margin        3435   4090.75  4862.425 5769.6091 18157.784
 11 Cumulative GPM             3435   7525.75 12388.175 18157.784
 12
 13 GPM as a % of Sales 0.2986957 0.3093195 0.3197123 0.3298793 0.3162065
 14 ----------------------------------------------------------------------
```

2. Position the cell pointer to row 2 and type

Keystroke	*Results*
I R	INSERT ROW # of rows: 1 before row: 2
Return	Completes Insert Row command.

3. Notice that a blank row is inserted at row 2.

4. Position the cell pointer to column 6 and type

Keystroke	*Results*
I C	INSERT COLUMN # of columns: 1 before column: 6
Return	Completes Insert Column command.

5. Notice that a blank column is inserted at column 6.

```
                    1                 2         3         4         5         6         7
  1                     Product Income and Cost Analysis
  2
  3 ------------------------------------------------------------           ----------
  4 Item                 1 Qtr     2 Qtr     3 Qtr     4 Qtr               Total
  5 ============================================================           ==========
  6 Sales                    11500     13225  15208.75 17490.063           57423.813
  7 Labor                     5620    6322.5 7112.8125 8001.9141           27057.227
  8 Material                  2445   2811.75 3233.5125 3718.5394           12208.802
  9 Total Cost                8065   9134.25 10346.325 11720.453           39266.028
 10 ============================================================           ==========
 11 Gross Profit Margin       3435   4090.75  4862.425 5769.6091           18157.784
 12 Cumulative GPM            3435   7525.75 12388.175 18157.784
 13
 14 GPM as a % of Sales 0.2986957 0.3093195 0.3197123 0.3298793           0.3162065
 15 ------------------------------------------------------------           ----------
```

6. To prevent overwriting the GPM.MP worksheet, which will be used again, Quit without saving by typing **Q N**; the operating system prompt is displayed.

Module 14
LOCK

DESCRIPTION

The Lock command, which can be thought of as a "protect" command, is used to prevent the destruction of cell contents by accidentally typing over a formula, number, or text. Data within locked cells can't be changed by the Alpha, Blank, Copy, Edit, Value, or Xternal commands. The form of the Lock command is

```
LOCK: Cells Formulas

Select option or type command letter
RnCn        Cell Contents          99% Free     Multiplan: FILENAME
```

All formula and text cells within a worksheet are simultaneously protected with the Lock Formulas command. Individual cells are protected or unprotected with the Lock Cells command. These command forms are explained in the following two paragraphs.

LOCK CELLS The form of the Lock Cells command is

```
LOCK cells: RnCn                status: Locked(Unlocked)

Enter reference to cell or group of cells
RnCn        Cell Contents          99% Free     Multiplan: FILENAME
```

To illustrate how to lock and unlock cells, an example is provided showing the keystrokes required to lock cell R8C4 and to unlock cell R7C3 of an active worksheet.

Lock cell R8C4 by positioning the cell pointer to R8C4 and typing

Keystrokes	*Results*	
L	LOCK: Cells Formulas	
C	LOCK cells: R8C4	status: Locked(Unlocked)
Tab L	LOCK cells: R8C4	status:(Locked)Unlocked
Return	Completes Lock Cell command	

Unlock cell R7C3 by positioning the cell pointer to R7C3 and typing

Keystrokes	*Results*	
L	LOCK: Cells Formulas	
C	LOCK cells: R7C3	status:(Locked)Unlocked
Tab U	LOCK cells: R8C4	status: Locked(Unlocked)
Return	Completes Lock Cell command	

If you want to unlock a group of cells or an entire worksheet, you can type a range of cells following the "LOCK cells:" selection. Typing R1:255 unlocks all cells; typing R3C2:5 unlocks the cells in row 3, columns 2 through 5.

In addition to locking and unlocking cells, you can use the Lock Cells command in conjunction with the cell pointer to determine if cells are locked or unlocked.

LOCK FORMULAS The form of the Lock Formulas command is

```
LOCK FORMULAS:

Enter Y to confirm
RnCn         Cell Contents          99% Free      Multiplan: FILENAME
```

To illustrate the Lock Formulas command, an example is provided showing the keystrokes required to lock all formulas and text within a worksheet. The position of the cell pointer is unimportant. To lock all formulas on an active worksheet, type

Keystrokes	*Results*
L	LOCK: Cells Formulas
F	LOCK FORMULAS:
Y	Responds to "Enter Y to confirm"; Completes Lock Formulas command

NEXT UNLOCKED CELL When you're using a worksheet containing locked cells, you can use the NEXT UNLOCKED CELL key (F5 or Ctrl-F) to jump the cell pointer to data entry cells. This is especially handy when entering numbers on large worksheets.

APPLICATIONS

The Lock command is extremely important when worksheets are designed for novice users. If cells are unlocked, it's possible for a beginning Multiplan user to type over formulas and destroy the integrity of the worksheet. Even experienced users sometimes forget and type over information that should be protected.

As you gain experience with worksheet design, you'll find that you can lay out your worksheets so that users can use the NEXT UNLOCKED CELL key to jump from one data entry cell to the next. This reduces the number of keystrokes and time required to enter data; more importantly, it reduces the possibility for errors.

TYPICAL OPERATION

In this illustration the Lock command is used to lock all cells containing formulas and text in the GPM.MP worksheet saved in Module 5, formatted in Module 10, and named in Module 18. Begin with Multiplan in the logged disk drive.

1. Type **MP GPM.MP** and press **Return** to display the GPM.MP worksheet. (If you saved GPM.MP on the diskette in drive B, use B:GPM.MP.) Notice the following display.

```
                  1                  2         3         4         5         6
 1                              Product Income and Cost Analysis
 2 ----------------------------------------------------------------------------
 3 Item                      1 Qtr     2 Qtr     3 Qtr     4 Qtr     Total
 4 ============================================================================
 5 Sales                 $11500.00 $13225.00 $15208.75 $17490.06 $57423.81
 6 Labor                  $5620.00  $6322.50  $7112.81  $8001.91 $27057.23
 7 Material               $2445.00  $2811.75  $3233.51  $3718.54 $12208.80
 8 Total Cost             $8065.00  $9134.25 $10346.33 $11720.45 $39266.03
 9 ============================================================================
10 Gross Profit Margin    $3435.00  $4090.75  $4862.43  $5769.61 $18157.78
11 Cumulative GPM         $3435.00  $7525.75 $12388.18 $18157.78
12
13 GPM as a % of Sales      29.87%    30.93%    31.97%    32.99%    31.62%
14 ----------------------------------------------------------------------------
```

NOTE

The following step is done just for practice, since the Lock Formulas command can be used to lock all formulas and text entries within the worksheet.

2. Lock cells R5C3 through R5C5 using the Lock Cell command as follows:
   a. Position the cell pointer to R5C3.
   b. Enter the following keystrokes:

Keystrokes	*Results*	
L	LOCK: Cells Formulas	
C	LOCK cells: R5C3	status: Locked(Unlocked)
:	LOCK cells: R5C3:	status: Locked(Unlocked)
Cell pointer to R5C5	LOCK cells: R5C3:R5C5	status: Locked(Unlocked)
Tab L	LOCK cells: R5C3:R5C5	status:(Locked)Unlocked
Return	Completes Lock Cell command	

3. Verify the lock status of cells R5C3 through R5C5 by typing

Keystrokes	Results	
L	LOCK: Cells Formulas	
C	LOCK cells: R5C3	status:(Locked)Unlocked
Cell pointer to R5C4	LOCK cells: R5C4	status:(Locked)Unlocked
Cell pointer to R5C5	LOCK cells: R5C5	status:(Locked)Unlocked
Return	Completes verification of locked cells	

The "(Locked)" display verifies that the selected cells are protected.

4. Lock all cells in the worksheet using the Lock Formulas command by typing

Keystrokes	*Results*
L	LOCK: Cells Formulas
F	LOCK FORMULAS:
Y	Responds to "Enter Y to confirm"; Completes Lock Formulas command

5. Now try to enter a number in a locked cell by positioning the cell pointer to cell R5C1, typing **123**, and pressing **Return**. Notice that text entry is disallowed. The message "Locked cells may not be changed" is displayed in the lower-left-hand corner of the screen.

6. Quit without saving by typing **Q N**; the operating system prompt is displayed.

Module 15

LOOKUP

DESCRIPTION

The lookup function is not a standard command, but it is an important operator with which you should become familiar. It lets you search through a table of values to find a specified match. The form for the lookup function is

LOOKUP(N,TABLE)

where N is a value to be looked up in the first row or column of a table. The table is a rectangular area in the active worksheet. When N is found, a corresponding value from the last row or column of the table is returned.

The dimensions of the table determine the direction lookup takes when it searches for the value N. If the table is square or has more rows than columns, values are searched in the first column. If the table is wider than it is long, values are searched in the first row. Lookup finds the largest value that is less than or equal to N.

The value N can be a row-column position or a named cell. The "TABLE" expression is a cell range, which includes the lookup column or row and the column or row of the table from which a value is returned. The value is returned to the cell containing the lookup formula.

A few simple examples are provided to illustrate the use of the lookup function. The two-column discount table that follows can be used to find the appropriate discount rate at different sales volumes.

	1	2	3	4
1	Units	Discount	Units --->	
2	0	0%	Discount->	
3	1	0%		
4	3	5%		
5	5	7%		
6	10	10%		
7				
8				

The setup for this worksheet is as follows:

1. Name cells R2C1 through R6C1 "Units."
2. Name cells R2C2 through R6C2 "Discount."
3. Name cell R1C4 "Number."
4. Enter the following formula in cell R2C4:

```
LOOKUP(NUMBER,UNITS:DISCOUNT)
```

To use the discount table, enter different numbers into cell R1C4 (to the right of "Units --->"). The appropriate discount rate is taken from the table opposite the specified unit value and displayed in cell R2C4 (to the right of "Discount->"). You may wish to use this example and enter different numbers in R1C4.

Multiple values can be extracted from a single lookup table by using several lookup formulas. Look at the following lookup table, used to compute fines and late charges that correspond to miles-per-hour in excess of the speed limit.

Excess Speed (C1)	*Fine* (C2)	*Late Charge* (C3)
0	0	0
5	25	10
10	50	15
15	75	20
20	100	25
25	200	30

Name the "Excess Speed" column C1, the "Fine" column C2, and the "Late Charge" column C3. The formula LOOKUP(20,C1:C2) returns the value 100 from column C2. The formula LOOKUP(20,C1:C3) returns the value 25 from column C3. Another example of a lookup table that uses values from two columns is illustrated in the Typical Operation section of this module.

APPLICATIONS

The lookup function can be applied to tax computations, discount schedules, grading, and late charges. As illustrated in the multiple-column lookup example, several values can be extracted from large lookup tables.

TYPICAL OPERATION

In this illustration the lookup function is used to compute a discount rate based on sales volume. Begin with Multiplan in the logged disk drive.

1. Type **MP** and press **Return** to display a blank worksheet.
2. Construct the following worksheet using the Alpha and Value commands.

```
           1          2          3
   1
   2
   3 Volume -->
   4 Discount:
   5                ----------
   6 Amt. Due
   7                ==========
   8
   9       Discount Rate Table
  10 VOLUME     MINIMUM    ADDER
  11          0          0          0
  12       5000        500        .05
  13      10000       1000        .06
  14      15000       1500        .07
  15      20000       2000        .08
  16      25000       2500        .09
  17      30000       3000         .1
```

3. Name the following cells with the specified names using the Name command.
   a. Cells R11C1:R17C1 - VOLUME
   b. Cells R11C2:R17C2 - MINIMUM
   c. Cells R11C3:R17C3 - ADDER
4. Enter the following formulas using the Value command.
   a. Cell R4C2: LOOKUP(R[– 1]C,VOLUME:MINIMUM) + (R[– 1]C – LOOKUP(R[– 1]C,VOLUME))* LOOKUP(R[– 1]C,VOLUME:ADDER)
   b. Cell R6C2: R[– 3]C – R[– 2]C
5. Format cells R3C2:R6C2 as dollars.
6. Format cells R11C3:R17C3 as percentages.

7. Enter 11000 in cell R3C2 and notice the following display.

```
             1          2          3
   1
   2
   3 Volume -->$11000.00
   4 Discount:   $1060.00
   5           ----------
   6 Amt. Due    $9940.00
   7           ==========
   8
   9       Discount Rate Table
  10 VOLUME    MINIMUM   ADDER
  11           0          0          0%
  12        5000        500          5%
  13       10000       1000          6%
  14       15000       1500          7%
  15       20000       2000          8%
  16       25000       2500          9%
  17       30000       3000         10%
```

8. Enter other volume values in cell R3C2 and notice the result.
9. If you wish to save this worksheet, use the Transfer Save command. Otherwise, use the Quit command to exit Multiplan.

Module 16
MACROS

DESCRIPTION

Multiplan version 2.0 introduced macros. A *macro* is a short-hand technique for giving instructions to your computer. It lets you prepare and store a long sequence of keystrokes that represent a series of commands into one or more worksheet cells. The Alpha mode is used to enter the information into the selected cell.

Once the instructions are entered, Multiplan's Name command is used to:

- Give the macro cell a name.
- Identify its row-column coordinates.
- Identify the named cell as a macro.
- Assign the macro a two-letter command key sequence.

The command key sequence is used to call the macro into action. This is done by pressing and holding **Alt** while the two keys are typed. Multiplan responds by using the stored instructions.

THE CONTENTS OF A MACRO

Macro cells are normally located in an out of the way place on your worksheet. If your sheet occupies an area ranging from R1C1 to R55C15, you might place your macro cells somewhere around R100C20.

Because you use the Alpha mode to enter commands into macro cells, you can enter letters, numbers, and punctuation marks. There are a number of special symbols that represent keystrokes and other useful instructions. For example, if 'tb is encountered in a macro, Multiplan interprets it as the **Tab** key. The sequence 'rt is interpreted as **Return**. The '? sequence causes Multiplan to wait for your input from the keyboard. When you press **Return**, control passes back to the instruction following the question mark, and the macro resumes operation.

Look at the following list of macro instructions. Notice that each begins with a single quote to tell Multiplan to interpret following characters as keystrokes or special instructions.

Key Codes:

Key	**Code**	**Key**	**Code**
Backspace	'bs	Previous field (backtab)	'pf
Character left	'cl	Page left	'pl
Cancel	'cn	Page right	'pr
Character right	'cr	Page up	'pu
Change window	'cw	Previous window	'pw
Down	'dk	Recalc	'rc
Delete	'dl	Reference	'rf
End	'en	Right	'rk
Help	'hp	Return	'rt
Home	'hm	Spacebar	'sp
Home window	'hw	Tab	'tb
Left	'lk	Up	'uk
Next unlocked cell	'nu	Word left	'wl
Previous unlocked cell	'pc	Word right	'wr
Page down	'pd	Accept keyboard input until Return key is pressed	'?

Command Codes:

Command	**Code**
Call a macro subroutine	'ca*RnCn*' ('re is used to return control back to calling macro)
Return to next instruction	're (only used with 'ca)
Go to next section of macro	'go*RnCn*'
Quit macro operation	'qu
Comment (language) in macro	'la*comment*'
Prompt user for alpha input at a specified cell	'al*prompt*'*RnCn*'
Prompt user for value input at a specified cell	'va*prompt*'*RnCn*'
Menu command with return	'mc*RnCn*' (returns to next instruction within calling macro)
Menu command without return	'mn*RnCn*'
Branch if condition is false	'if*condition*' (if not false, control moves to next instruction)

General Notes:

1. You can press Ctrl-V and press a key like Tab or Return to enter 'tb or 'rt automatically. An "EM" is displayed at the bottom of your screen. This stands for *edit macro*.
2. Do not enter spaces within macro strings except in comments and prompts.
3. All command codes are preceded with an apostrophe.

EXAMPLE 1 This is a simple macro used to load files from your logged disk. If you wish, follow along on your computer to see how to create, name, and run this macro. Begin with a clear Multiplan screen.

1. Type **GR50**, press **Tab**, type **20**, and press **Return** to Goto cell R50C20.
2. Type **A** to select Alpha and type the macro text into cell R50C20 exactly as shown. Then press **Return**.

NOTE

Remember, you can use **Ctrl-V** to turn edit macro on. Instead of typing 'dk and 'rt, you can press the **Down Arrow** and **Return** keys. Be sure to press **Ctrl-V** again to turn edit macro off. Otherwise, all keystrokes are interpreted as key codes.

```
#1        15        19        20        21
  49
  50                        tl'dk'?'rt
```

This macro string is defined as:

t	l	'dk	'?	'rt
Transfer	Load	DownKey	(input)	Return

3. With the cell pointer still in R50C20, use Name to name the cell as a macro with the following keystrokes:

Keystrokes	*Results*
N	define name:
getfile	define name: getfile
Tab	to refer to: R50C20
Tab Y	macro:(Yes)No
Tab	command key(s):
gf	command key(s): gf

When your name screen looks like the following one, press **Return**.

```
NAME: define name: getfile            to refer to: R50C20
      macro:(Yes)No                   command key(s): gf

R50C20    "tl'dk'?'rt"                 100% Free     Multiplan: MACRO#1.MP
```

4. Run the macro by pressing **Alt-GF**. Notice that the question mark passes control back to you for input from the keyboard. Once you select a file, pressing **Return** transfers control back to the macro and the selected file loads.

EXAMPLE 2 This example shows you how to prepare a macro that displays a Multiplan formatting menu with corresponding screen messages. Before creating the macro, a simple worksheet is prepared that is used to demonstrate the power of the macro.

1. Display a clear worksheet and enter the headings and values shown below.

```
#1     1    2    3    4    5    6    7
  1           Sales for First Half
  2  Jan   Feb   Mar   Apr   May   Jun  Total
  3 -----------------------------------------
  4   1.6   1.6   1.6   1.6   1.6   1.6   9.3
  5   2.3   2.3   2.3   2.3   2.3   2.3  14.0
  6   1.7   1.7   1.7   1.7   1.7   1.7  10.0
  7 -----------------------------------------
```

2. Move the cell pointer to R100C20.
3. Use Alpha to type in the macro instructions and text shown in the range of cells beginning with R100C20 and ending with R103C20. Do not type in the explanatory remarks.

Row Column		*Remarks (Do not type)*
#1	20	
99		
100	'mnr101c20	Menu at R101C20
101	Left	Displays "Left"
102	Set text flush left in cell(s)	User message
103	fc:'?'tbl'rt	Macro definition: Format Cell (input) Tab Left Return
104		

4. Use Alpha to type in the macro instructions and text in cells R101C21 through R103C25 as shown. Do not type in the explanatory remarks to the right of each entry.

#1	21	
100		
101	Center	Displays "Center"
102	Center text	User message
103	fc:'?'tbc'rt	Macro definition: Format Cell (input) Tab Center Return
104		

#1 22	
100	
101 Right	Displays "Right"
102 Set text flush right	User message
103 fc:'?'tbr'rt	Macro definition: Format Cell (input)Tab Right Return
104	

#1 23	
100	
101 Decimal	Displays "Decimal"
102 Format numbers as decimals	User message
103 fc:'?'tb'tbf'tb1'rt	Macro definition: Format Cell (input) Tab Tab Fix Tab 1 Return
104	

#1 24	
100	
101 Dollar	Displays "Dollar"
102 Format numbers in dollars	User message
103 fc:'?'tb'tb$'rt	Macro definition: Format Cell (input) Tab Tab $ Return
104	

#1 25	
100	
101 Percent	Displays "Percent"
102 Format numbers as percent	User message
103 fc:'?'tb'tb%'rt	Macro definition: Format Cell (input) Tab Tab % Return
104	

5. When you finish, the macro area resembles the following illustration. Notice that you cannot see the entire user messages or macro instructions. To check them, position the cell pointer and use Edit.

```
#1      20       21       22       23       24       25
 99
 100 'mnr101c20
 101 Left      Center    Right     Decimal   Dollar    Percent
 102 Set text fCenter texSet text fFormat numFormat numFormat num
 103 fc:'?'tbl'fc:'?'tbc'fc:'?'tbr'fc:'?'tb'tfc:'?'tb'tfc:'?'tb't
 104
```

6. Move the cell pointer to R100C20.

7. Use Name to name the cell as a macro with the following keystrokes:

Keystrokes	*Results*
N	define name:
format	define name: format
Tab	to refer to: R50C20
Tab Y	macro:(Yes)No
Tab	command key(s):
fc	command key(s): fc

When your name screen looks like the following one, press **Return**.

```
NAME: define name: format          to refer to: R100C20
      macro:(Yes)No                command key(s): fc
```

8. Press **Home** to move the cell pointer to R1C1.
9. Press **Alt-FC** to run the macro. Experiment with the format commands offered by the macro. Use the cell pointer to select different ranges of cells affected by the format operations. You may wish to save the worksheet for reference.

EXAMPLE 3 This example creates a worksheet from scratch. It is designed to show you how a macro can use subroutines. Here, the same subroutine is called twice to draw horizontal lines. Once the worksheet is created, the user is prompted to enter quarterly sales figures.

1. Begin work in a clear worksheet.
2. Move the cell pointer to R50C20.
3. Use Alpha to type the macro instructions in the indicated cells. A macro definition is provided for each entry.

Text within cells and prompts are surrounded by double quotes for clarification within the macro definitions.

R50C20
'hmfw15'rtaDescription'rkQtr 1'rkQtr 2'rkQtr 3'rkQtr 4'rkTotal'rt'gor52c20'rt

Macro definition:

Home Format Width 15 Return Alpha "Description" RightKey "Qtr 1" RightKey "Qtr 2" RightKey "Qtr 3" RightKey "Qtr 4" RightKey "Total" Return GoR52C20 Return

R51C20
gr2'tb1'rt'caR55C20'gr1'tb2'rtfc:R1C6'tbr'rt'caR53C20'rt

Macro definition:

Goto Row 2 Tab 1 Return Call R55C20 Goto Row 1 Tab 2 Return Format Cell : R1C6 Tab Right Return Call R53C20 Return

R52C20
gr3'tb1'rtaNuts'dkBolts'dkWashers'rtgr3'tb6'rtvSUM('lk'lk'lk'lk:'lk)'rtcd2'rt'goR54C20

Macro definition:

Goto Row 3 Tab 1 Return Alpha "Nuts" DownKey "Bolts" DownKey "Washers" Return Goto Row 3 Tab 6 Return Value SUM(LeftKey LeftKey LeftKey LeftKey : LeftKey) Return Copy Down 2 Return Go R54C20

R53C20
gr6'tb1'rt'car55c20'gr7'tb2'rtvSUM('uk'uk'uk'uk:'uk'uk)'rtcr4'rt'va Enter quarterly sales figures'R3C2' qu

Macro definition:

Goto Row 6 Tab 1 Return Call R55C20 Goto Row 7 Tab 2 Return Value SUM(UpKey UpKey UpKey UpKey : UpKey UpKey) Return Copy Right 4 Return ValuePrompt "Enter quarterly sales figures"R3C2 Quit

R54C20
a--------------'rtcr5'rt're

Macro definition (This is the subroutine.):

Alpha "---------------" Return Copy Right 5 Return (return to call)

4. Check your screen for the following display. Use the edit function to proofread your work within each macro cell.

```
#1          20          21
  49
  50  'hmfw15'rt
  51  gr2'tbl'rt
  52  gr3'tbl'rt
  53  gr6'tbl'rt
  54  a---------
  55
```

5. Move the cell pointer to R50C20.

6. Use Name to name the cell as a macro with the following keystrokes:

Keystrokes	*Results*
N	define name:
make	define name: make
Tab	to refer to: R50C20
Tab Y	macro:(Yes)No
Tab	command key(s):
mm	command key(s): mm

When your name screen looks like the following one, press **Return**.

```
NAME: define name: make                          to refer to: R50C20
      macro:(Yes)No                              command key(s): mm
```

7. Run the macro by pressing **Alt-MM**.
8. Notice that the entire worksheet is created. The resulting worksheet resembles the following one.

```
#1         1                2          3          4          5          6
  1 Description          Qtr 1      Qtr 2      Qtr 3      Qtr 4      Total
  2 ------------------------------------------------------------------------
  3 Nuts                 4.333      4.333      4.333      4.333     17.332
  4 Bolts                3.555      3.555      3.555      3.555      14.22
  5 Washers              1.666      1.666      1.666      1.666      6.664
  6 ------------------------------------------------------------------------
  7                      9.554      9.554      9.554      9.554     38.216
```

If you encounter problems, press the **End** key to jump the cell pointer back to the macro area and check your macro instructions for accuracy.

APPLICATIONS

The macro instruction capability is a powerful tool. It lets experienced Multiplan users prepare complex worksheets for inexperienced ones. You can also create a set of useful macro tools that let you perform complex operations with a few easy keystrokes. For example, you can build a set of macros similar to the ones in Examples 1 and 2 for formatting, file handling, and so on.

If you are the "house" worksheet programmer (or want to be one), you can build macros to simplify data entry for frequently used worksheets. For example, when financial reports are changed each month, you can build a macro to:

1. Summarize prior financial periods.
2. Delete detail that is no longer required in the current report.
3. Prompt the user to enter current and forecast figures.
4. Add the current and future forecast figures.
5. Produce a printed report.

Although it may take several hours to prepare such a macro, you may realize a substantial long-term savings. This is especially true if many worksheet users are involved.

Another benefit is the quality. The macro simplifies the data entry process, which assures an increased level in the reliability of financial information.

TYPICAL OPERATION

In this illustration the macro function is used to load a file from disk. Begin by loading the Multiplan program.

1. Type **MP** and press **Return** to display a blank worksheet.
2. Type **GR50**, press **Tab**, type **20**, and press **Return** to Goto cell R50C20.
3. Type **A** to select Alpha and type the macro text into cell R50C20 exactly as shown. Press **Return**.

```
#1       15       19       20       21
  49
  50                    tl'dk'?'rt
```

4. With the cell pointer still in R50C20, use Name to name the cell as a macro with the following keystrokes:

Keystrokes	*Results*
N	define name:
getfile	define name: getfile
Tab	to refer to: R50C20
Tab Y	macro:(Yes)No
Tab	command key(s):
gf	command key(s): gf

When your name screen looks like the following one, press **Return**.

```
NAME: define name: getfile                 to refer to: R50C20
      macro:(Yes)No                        command key(s): gf

R50C20    "tl'dk'?'rt"                 100% Free     Multiplan: MACRO#1.MP
```

5. Run the macro by pressing **Alt-GF**. Select a worksheet file with the cursor and press **Return** to load it. Quit Multiplan by typing **Q Y**.

Module 17

MOVE

DESCRIPTION

The Move command is used to relocate one or more entire rows or columns from one location of the active worksheet to another. The form for the Move command is

```
MOVE: Row Column

Select option or type command letter
RnCn        Cell Contents          99% Free     Multiplan: FILENAME
```

The following two paragraph sections describe the Move Row and Move Column commands. If you wish, you can follow along on your computer.

MOVE ROW Two examples of the Move Row command are described. The first moves a single row, while the second moves three rows. To move row 7 above row 3, position the cell pointer to row 7 and type

Keystrokes	*Results*		
M R	MOVE ROW from rows: 7	to before row: 7	# of rows: 1
Tab 3	MOVE ROW from rows: 7	to before row: 3	# of rows: 1
Return	Completes Move Row command.		

To move rows 7, 8, and 9 above row 3, position the cell pointer to row 7 and type

Keystrokes	*Results*		
M R	MOVE ROW from rows: 7	to before row: 7	# of rows: 1
Tab 3	MOVE ROW from rows: 7	to before row: 3	# of rows: 1
Tab 3	MOVE ROW from rows: 7	to before row: 3	# of rows: 3
Return	Completes Move Row command.		

MOVE COLUMN Two examples of the Move Column command are described. The first moves a single column and the second moves three columns.

To move column 7 to the left of column 3, position the cell pointer to column 7 and type

Keystrokes	*Results*		
M C	MOVE COLUMN from columns: 7	to left of column: 7	# of columns: 1
Tab 3	MOVE COLUMN from columns: 7	to left of column: 3	# of columns: 1
Return	Completes Move Column command.		

To move columns 7, 8, and 9 to the left of column 3, position the cell pointer to column 7 and type

Keystrokes	*Results*		
M R	MOVE COLUMN from columns: 7	to left of column: 7	# of columns: 1
Tab 3	MOVE COLUMN from columns: 7	to left of column: 3	# of columns: 1
Tab 3	MOVE COLUMN from columns: 7	to left of column: 3	# of columns: 3
Return	Completes Move Column command.		

When relative values are used, Multiplan adds the rows or columns necessary to maintain formula integrity. However, with absolute cell addresses, the Move command should be used sparingly, as you may be required to edit cell references within your formulas. If cell names are used, as described in Module 18, the Move command won't affect cell references in these formulas.

APPLICATIONS

As you design a worksheet, you'll often find that you want to rearrange one or more rows or columns. This makes the Move command a handy tool. There is an alternative to Move – the Insert, Copy, and Delete commands can be used to move (or relocate) cells. In fact, because the Move command relocates entire rows or columns, the only way to relocate a series of cells is to insert blank cells into the target cell area, copy the source cells into the target area, and then delete the original source cells.

TYPICAL OPERATION

In this illustration the Move command is used to move a row between the title of the GPM.MP worksheet and the first horizontal rule in row 2. Begin with Multiplan in the logged disk drive, and load the GPM.MP worksheet saved in Module 5.

1. Type **MP GPM.MP** and press **Return** to display the GPM.MP worksheet. (If you saved GPM.MP on the diskette in drive B, use B:GPM.MP.) Notice the following display.

```
              1              2          3          4          5          6
 1                    Product Income and Cost Analysis
 2 ------------------------------------------------------------------------
 3 Item                   1 Qtr      2 Qtr      3 Qtr      4 Qtr      Total
 4 ========================================================================
 5 Sales                  11500      13225   15208.75  17490.063  57423.813
 6 Labor                   5620     6322.5  7112.8125  8001.9141  27057.227
 7 Material                2445    2811.75  3233.5125  3718.5394  12208.802
 8 Total Cost              8065    9134.25  10346.325  11720.453  39266.028
 9 ========================================================================
10 Gross Profit Margin     3435    4090.75   4862.425  5769.6091  18157.784
11 Cumulative GPM          3435    7525.75  12388.175  18157.784
12
13 GPM as a % of Sales 0.2986957 0.3093195 0.3197123 0.3298793 0.3162065
14 ------------------------------------------------------------------------
```

2. Position the cell pointer to row 12 and type

Keystrokes	*Results*
M R	MOVE ROW from rows: 12 to before row: 12 # of rows: 1
Tab 2	MOVE ROW from rows: 12 to before row: 2 # of rows: 1
Return	Completes Move Row command.

3. Notice that row 12 is moved above row 2.

```
              1              2          3          4          5          6
 1                    Product Income and Cost Analysis
 2
 3 ------------------------------------------------------------------------
 4 Item                   1 Qtr      2 Qtr      3 Qtr      4 Qtr      Total
 5 ========================================================================
 6 Sales                  11500      13225   15208.75  17490.063  57423.813
 7 Labor                   5620     6322.5  7112.8125  8001.9141  27057.227
 8 Material                2445    2811.75  3233.5125  3718.5394  12208.802
 9 Total Cost              8065    9134.25  10346.325  11720.453  39266.028
10 ========================================================================
11 Gross Profit Margin     3435    4090.75   4862.425  5769.6091  18157.784
12 Cumulative GPM          3435    7525.75  12388.175  18157.784
13 GPM as a % of Sales 0.2986957 0.3093195 0.3197123 0.3298793 0.3162065
14 ------------------------------------------------------------------------
```

4. To prevent overwriting the GPM.MP worksheet, which will be used again, quit without saving by typing **Q N**; the operating system prompt is displayed.

Module 18

NAME

DESCRIPTION

The Name command is used to assign a natural language name to one or more cells. For example, if you have a cell labeled "TOTAL," you may wish to assign "TOTAL" as a name. If you have a row of cells containing assets, you can assign the name "ASSETS" to the entire row. Once the row has been named, the formula SUM(ASSETS) yields the sum of all numbers in the ASSETS row. An entire worksheet table consisting of a rectangular area of cells can also be named. You can name cells either before or after formulas or text are entered.

The form of the Name command is

```
NAME: define name:                  to refer to: RnCn

Enter name
RnCn         Cell Contents           99% Free     Multiplan: FILENAME
```

Names may contain up to 31 characters. They must start with an alphabetical character but may contain numbers and underscores. Illegal characters are ignored; underscores may be substituted for spaces between words in a name. If you want to check existing names, you can activate the Name command by typing **N** and pressing the cursor keys to display names and corresponding cells. To discontinue this process, simply press **Esc** to return to the command line. To illustrate the use of the Name command, a cell and a row are assigned a name in the following examples.

NAMING A CELL In this example a cell is given the name "Subtotal." Begin by positioning the cell pointer to the desired cell–say R9C3–and type

Keystrokes	*Results*	
N	NAME: define name:	to refer to: R9C3
Subtotal	NAME: define name: Subtotal	to refer to: R9C3
Return	Completes Name command	

To delete a name, enter the name following the "define name:" prompt, delete the response following the "to refer to:" prompt, and press **Return**.

NAMING A SERIES OF CELLS In this example a row of cells is given the name "Asset Row." Begin by positioning the cell pointer to the leftmost cell, say R5C2, and type

Keystrokes	*Results*	
N	NAME: define name:	to refer to: R5C2
Asset_Row	NAME: define name: Asset_Row	to refer to: R5C2
Tab :	NAME: define name: Asset_Row	to refer to: R5C2:
Cell Pointer to R5C5	NAME: define name: Asset_Row	to refer to: R5C2:R5C5
Return	Completes Name command	

USING NAMES IN FORMULAS Once a cell or series of cells is named, you can use the name in a formula instead of an absolute or relative cell reference. For example, a formula that adds the values in the range of cells named "Asset_Row" in the previous paragraph in cell R5C6 is written

```
VALUE: SUM(Asset_Row)

Enter a formula
R5C6                              99% Free     Multiplan: FILENAME
```

APPLICATIONS

The Name command is an excellent way to organize a worksheet by assigning meaningful names to cells, rows, columns, or tables. Names stay with a cell or series of cells; therefore, inserting or deleting areas within a worksheet doesn't affect formulas containing relative references to named cells.

Naming cells is also convenient when a cell or series of cells in one worksheet is used by another. This process is described in Module 26, where the External command is explained.

TYPICAL OPERATION

In this illustration the Name command is used to name the "Sales," "Labor," "Material," and "Total Cost" cells in the GPM.MP worksheet created in Module 5 and formatted in Module 10. Once the cells are named, the formulas in the Total column are rewritten to use the cell names. Begin with Multiplan in the logged disk drive.

1. Type **MP GPM.MP** and press **Return** to display the GPM.MP worksheet. (If you saved GPM.MP on the diskette in drive B, use B:GPM.MP.) Notice the following display.

```
                        1          2         3         4         5         6
 1                              Product Income and Cost Analysis
 2 ----------------------------------------------------------------------
 3 Item                      1 Qtr     2 Qtr     3 Qtr     4 Qtr     Total
 4 ======================================================================
 5 Sales                 $11500.00 $13225.00 $15208.75 $17490.06 $57423.81
 6 Labor                  $5620.00  $6322.50  $7112.81  $8001.91 $27057.23
 7 Material               $2445.00  $2811.75  $3233.51  $3718.54 $12208.80
 8 Total Cost             $8065.00  $9134.25 $10346.33 $11720.45 $39266.03
 9 ======================================================================
10 Gross Profit Margin    $3435.00  $4090.75  $4862.43  $5769.61 $18157.78
11 Cumulative GPM         $3435.00  $7525.75 $12388.18 $18157.78
12
13 GPM as a % of Sales      29.87%    30.93%    31.97%    32.99%    31.62%
14 ----------------------------------------------------------------------
```

2. Assign the name "Sales" to columns 2 through 5 of row 5 as follows:
   a. Position the cell pointer to R5C2.
   b. Enter the following keystrokes:

Keystrokes	*Results*	
N	NAME: define name:	to refer to: R5C2
Sales	NAME: define name: Sales	to refer to: R5C2
Tab :	NAME: define name: Sales	to refer to: R5C2:
Cell Pointer to R5C5	NAME: define name: Sales	to refer to: R5C2:R5C5
Return	Completes Name command	

3. Assign the name "Labor" to columns 2 through 5 of row 6 as follows:
   a. Position the cell pointer to R6C2.
   b. Enter the following keystrokes:

Keystrokes	*Results*	
N	NAME: define name:	to refer to: R6C2
Labor	NAME: define name: Labor	to refer to: R6C2
Tab :	NAME: define name: Labor	to refer to: R6C2:
Cell Pointer to R6C5	NAME: define name: Labor	to refer to: R6C2:R6C5
Return	Completes Name command	

4. Assign the name "Material" to columns 2 through 5 of row 7 as follows:
   a. Position the cell pointer to R7C2.
   b. Enter the following keystrokes:

Keystrokes	*Results*	
N	NAME: define name:	to refer to: R7C2
Material	NAME: define name: Material	to refer to: R7C2
Tab :	NAME: define name: Material	to refer to: R7C2:
Cell Pointer to R7C5	NAME: define name: Material	to refer to: R7C2:R7C5
Return	Completes Name command	

5. Assign the name "Cost" to columns 2 through 5 of row 8 as follows:
   a. Position the cell pointer to R8C2.
   b. Enter the following keystrokes:

Keystrokes	*Results*	
N	NAME: define name:	to refer to: R8C2
Cost	NAME: define name: Cost	to refer to: R8C2
Tab :	NAME: define name: Cost	to refer to: R8C2:
Cell Pointer to R8C5	NAME: define name: Cost	to refer to: R8C2:R8C5
Return	Completes Name command	

6. Assign the name "Total_Sales" to cell R5C6 as follows:
   a. Position the cell pointer to R5C6.
   b. Enter the following keystrokes:

Keystrokes	*Results*	
N	NAME: define name:	to refer to: R5C6
Total_Sales	NAME: define name: Total_Sales	to refer to: R5C6
Return	Completes Name command	

7. Assign the name "Total_Cost" to cell R8C6 as follows:
   a. Position the cell pointer to R8C6.
   b. Enter the following keystrokes:

Keystrokes	*Results*	
N	NAME: define name:	to refer to: R8C6
Total_Cost	NAME: define name: Total_Cost	to refer to: R8C6
Return	Completes Name command	

8. Use the Value command to rewrite the formulas in column 6 as shown in the following list.

Cell	*Formula*
R5C6	SUM(Sales)
R6C6	SUM(Labor)
R7C6	SUM(Material)
R8C6	SUM(Cost)
	==========
R10C6	Total_Sales-Total_Cost

9. Notice that all values are still intact after use of the Name command.
10. Save the worksheet by typing **T S** for Transfer Save, press **Return**, and type **Y** for Yes.
11. Quit by typing **Q** for Quit; the operating system prompt is displayed.

Module 19

OPTIONS

DESCRIPTION

The Options command is used to perform the following three functions:

- Turn automatic recalculation on and off.
- Turn the computer's speaker on and off.
- Set up Multiplan to perform iterative (circular) calculations.

The form of the Options command is:

```
OPTIONS recalc: Yes No         mute: Yes(No)
        iteration: Yes(No)     completion test at:
Select option
RnCn        Cell Contents              99% Free      Multiplan: FILENAME
```

The functions of the Options command are described in the following paragraphs.

RECALC The Options Recalc command lets you turn off automatic recalculation to avoid calculation delays each time you enter or change a number in your worksheet. When recalculation is off, you can enter numbers and text as usual, but answers are not affected until you press the **RECALCULATE** key (**!**). When a formula is copied, the displayed value is also transferred. The correct value replaces the displayed value when you press **RECALCULATE**.

Automatic recalculation is normally on. To turn it off, type

Keystrokes	*Results*	
O	OPTIONS recalc: Yes No	mute: Yes(No)
N	OPTIONS recalc: Yes(No)	mute: Yes(No)
Return	Completes Options Recalc command	

To turn automatic recalculation back on, type

Keystrokes	*Results*	
O	OPTIONS recalc: Yes(No)	mute: Yes(No)
Y	OPTIONS recalc:(Yes)No	mute: Yes(No)
Return	Completes Options Recalc command	

OPTIONS MUTE The Options Mute command turns your computer's speaker on and off. The normal setting is "No," which causes the speaker to "beep" when an entry error is detected. If you want to turn the "beep" off when entry errors are detected, you can set mute to "Yes" by typing

Keystrokes	*Results*	
O	OPTIONS recalc:(Yes)No	mute: Yes(No)
Tab Y	OPTIONS recalc:(Yes)No	mute:(Yes)No
Return	Completes Options Mute command	

ITERATION The Options Iteration and Completion Test At commands work together as a pair with iterative, or "circular-type," formulas. An iterative formula is one that has two or more mutually dependent elements. When one element changes, a second element is changed. It may be increased (incremented) or decreased (decremented) in value. When the second element changes, it causes the initial element to change, going full circle. Hence the expression *iterative* or *circular*.

If it is left unchecked, the circular process runs away. This is where the Options Completion Test At command comes into play. An iteration count is established within a designated cell using the ITERCNT( ) operator. If ITERCNT( ) = 1, only one iteration at a time occurs. The ITERCNT( ) operator can be adjusted as required.

A simple example of an iterative formula is shown to illustrate how iteration works. Before entering the values, set up Multiplan for iteration by typing

Keystrokes	*Results*	
O	OPTIONS recalc:(Yes)No	mute: Yes(No)
Tab Tab	iteration: Yes(No)	completion test at:
Y	iteration:(Yes)No	completion test at:
Tab R1C1	iteration:(Yes)No	completion test at: R1C1
Return	Completes Options Iteration command	

In addition to the ITERCNT( ) operator, the DELTA( ) operator is also within a logical IF formula. Using the cell pointer and the Value command, enter the following formulas beginning with cell R1C1.

Cell	*Formula*
R1C1	ITERCNT( )=5
R2C1	R3C1
R3C1	R2C1+1
R4C1	IF(TRUE( ),DELTA( ),“ ”)

Press **RECALC** (!) and notice the display. The value 1 is the difference (DELTA) between R2C1 and R3C1.

The value in R2C1 is equal to the value of R3C1, which in turn is equal to the value of R2C1 plus 1. Thus the two cells are dependent upon each other. Without iteration count control established in R1C1, the values in both cells would begin to increment out of control. However, the iteration count is set to 5, which allows only five iterations to occur. Subsequent iterations are achieved by pressing the **RECALC** key (!).

The values associated with the initial setting (0) and four iterations are shown in the following list.

Iteration	*Cell R2C1*	*Cell R3C1*	*Cell R4C1*
0	0	1	1
1	6	7	1
2	12	13	1
3	18	19	1
4	24	25	1

The DELTA( ) operator is used to evaluate the difference between the two values. In the example, that difference is 1. If the formula in cell R3C1 is changed to R2C1 + 2, the difference displayed in R4C1 is 2. The DELTA( ) value is displayed when the completion test cell is TRUE. If the completion test is FALSE, a blank (" ") is displayed.

In financial models that use iteration, the DELTA( ) value sometimes converges (the difference is reduced with each iteration). At other times, the difference may increase (or diverge). The DELTA( ) operator can be used as a test to determine when the difference reaches a certain limit. For example, the formula DELTA( )<1 returns a TRUE value when the difference between the previous result and the current result is less than 1.

If the Iteration command is set to "No," iterative calculations cannot occur, and the message "Circular references unresolved" appears in the lower-left-hand corner of the screen.

APPLICATIONS

The most commonly used Options command is the Options Recalc command, used to suppress automatic recalculation. Turning off automatic recalculation speeds up data entry. The improvement is more noticeable on large worksheets, where recalculation may take up to several seconds. Delays from automatic recalculation on small worksheets are normally not bothersome.

The Options Mute command is normally set to eliminate the "beep" caused by error detection. This prevents the speaker tone from annoying others in a work area. However, if entry errors are critical, it may be desirable to turn the muting off.

The Options Iterative and Completion Test At commands are used in conjunction with iterative models to test different assumptions. For examples of iterative models, refer to your Multiplan documentation.

TYPICAL OPERATION

In this illustration the Options Recalc command is used to turn off automatic recalculation of the GPM.MP worksheet saved in Module 5, formatted in Module 10, and named in Module 18. New numbers are entered into rows 5 through 7 of column 2 and then the **RECALC** key is pressed to display new answers. Begin with Multiplan in the logged disk drive.

1. Type **MP GPM.MP** and press **Return** to display the GPM.MP worksheet. (If you saved GPM.MP on the diskette in drive B, use B:GPM.MP.) Notice the following display.

```
                 1          2         3         4         5         6
  1                     Product Income and Cost Analysis
  2 ----------------------------------------------------------------------
  3 Item                  1 Qtr     2 Qtr     3 Qtr     4 Qtr     Total
  4 ======================================================================
  5 Sales              $11500.00 $13225.00 $15208.75 $17490.06 $57423.81
  6 Labor               $5620.00  $6322.50  $7112.81  $8001.91 $27057.23
  7 Material            $2445.00  $2811.75  $3233.51  $3718.54 $12208.80
  8 Total Cost          $8065.00  $9134.25 $10346.33 $11720.45 $39266.03
  9 ======================================================================
 10 Gross Profit Margin $3435.00  $4090.75  $4862.43  $5769.61 $18157.78
 11 Cumulative GPM      $3435.00  $7525.75 $12388.18 $18157.78
 12
 13 GPM as a % of Sales   29.87%    30.93%    31.97%    32.99%    31.62%
 14 ----------------------------------------------------------------------
```

2. Turn off automatic recalculation by typing

Keystrokes	*Results*	
O	OPTIONS recalc: Yes No	mute: Yes(No)
N	OPTIONS recalc: Yes(No)	mute: Yes(No)
Return	Completes Options Recalc command	

3. Using the cell pointer and the Value command, enter the following values:

Cell	*Value*
R5C2	10000
R6C2	4800
R7C2	2975

4. Notice that the worksheet answers are unaffected as the new numbers are entered.
5. Press the **RECALC** key (!) and notice that the answers are displayed as shown in the following worksheet.

```
                     1              2          3          4          5          6
 1                          Product Income and Cost Analysis
 2 ------------------------------------------------------------------------
 3 Item                        1 Qtr      2 Qtr      3 Qtr      4 Qtr      Total
 4 ========================================================================
 5 Sales                  $10000.00 $11500.00 $13225.00 $15208.75 $49933.75
 6 Labor                   $4800.00  $5400.00  $6075.00  $6834.38 $23109.38
 7 Material                $2975.00  $3421.25  $3934.44  $4524.60 $14855.29
 8 Total Cost              $7775.00  $8821.25 $10009.44 $11358.98 $37964.67
 9 ========================================================================
10 Gross Profit Margin     $2225.00  $2678.75  $3215.56  $3849.77 $11969.08
11 Cumulative GPM         $2225.00  $4903.75  $8119.31 $11969.08
12
13 GPM as a % of Sales       22.25%    23.29%    24.31%    25.31%    23.97%
14 ------------------------------------------------------------------------
```

6. Quit without saving by typing **Q N**; the operating system prompt is displayed.

Module 20

PRINT

DESCRIPTION

The Print command is used to print your worksheets to your printer or to a disk file. The Print command offers a generous number of formatting selections. You can print a selected portion of your worksheet; adjust margins, page width, and page length; include row and column numbers on your printout; print formulas instead of values; and send control codes to your printer for turning on variations such as compressed print and underscore.

The form for the Print command is

```
PRINT: Printer File Margins Options

Select option or type command letter
RnCn         Cell Contents          99% Free     Multiplan: FILENAME
```

The following four paragraphs within this section describe the Printer, File, Margins, and Options selections.

PRINTER The Print command is started by typing **P**. This displays the main set of Print command selections. You'll notice that "Printer" is highlighted, which means that pressing **Return** starts the printing process. However, before you press **Return**, you'll want to check your margins by typing **M** to display the "Margins" selections. You'll also want to check your worksheet size and printer setup by typing **O** to display the "Options" selections. Both of these subcommands are explained in this section.

FILE The Print File command is selected by typing **P F**. The following prompts are displayed.

```
PRINT on file:

Enter a filename
RnCn         Cell Contents          99% Free     Multiplan: FILENAME
```

Typing a filename and pressing **Return** transfers the worksheet to a standard text file on the logged (active) disk drive. You may prefix the filename with a drive specification, such as B:FILENAME, to write the file to the diskette in drive B. As in printing, however, before you save the worksheet to a text file, use the "Margins" and "Options" selections to be sure that the margins and worksheet dimensions are satisfactory.

MARGINS The Print Margins command is selected by typing **P M**. The resulting selections are displayed.

```
PRINT MARGINS: left: 5     top: 6     print width: 70     print length: 54
               page length: 66
Enter a number
RnCn        Cell Contents          99% Free     Multiplan: FILENAME
```

Margins are adjusted by entering the appropriate number following each selection. You can move between selections by pressing the **Tab** key.

Horizontal Measure The left margin (left:) and print width selections are measured in characters. If you have a 10-character-per-inch printer, the left margin will be ½ inch wide with a setting of 5. The print width will be 7 inches with a setting of 70. If you're using compressed print, which is typically 17 characters per inch, you'll want to use a left margin of 9 to obtain a ½-inch left margin, and a print width of 119 for a 7-inch-wide printed area. In both of these setups, your left- and right-hand margins will be approximately ½ inch.

Vertical Measure The "top:," print length:," and "page length:" selections are measured in lines (or line feeds). Because a printer uses six lines per inch, a top margin setting of 6 provides a one-inch space at the top of your printed worksheet. A print length of 54 lines yields a 10-inch-long printed worksheet area. A 66-line page length causes a form-feed every 11 inches. This is consistent with standard 8½-by-11-inch cut sheets and continuous-form paper.

Print Setting	*1-Inch Margins*	*6.5-Inch Print Width*
5 cpi	5	32*
10 cpi	10	65
12 cpi	12	78
17 cpi	17	110*

* Approximate

If you plan to print on cut-sheet paper, your worksheet area should never exceed 66 lines, including top margin and print length. Otherwise, you'll be printing on your printer platen.

OPTIONS The Print Options command is selected by typing **P O**. The following selections are displayed.

```
PRINT OPTIONS: area: R1:4095          setup:
               formulas: Yes(No)      row-col numbers: Yes(No)
Enter a number
RnCn        Cell Contents             99% Free     Multiplan: FILENAME
```

You can move between Print Option command selections with the **Tab** key. The selections are explained below.

Area: The "area:" selection lets you choose the size of the worksheet area to be printed. The default R1:4095 selects the entire worksheet, including columns 1 through 255. However, Multiplan only prints columns occupied with data. Therefore, you won't have to worry about blank columns outside the worksheet area.

If you attempt to print an area wider than the print width, the portion of the worksheet to the right of the print width is printed on the second printed page. Extremely wide worksheets may be printed in several "strips."

Setup: The "setup:" selection allows you to enter printer control codes that switch on special printing. These codes vary between printers. A few common control codes are shown in the following list, although you should consult your printer manual to determine which control codes are appropriate for your printer.

Function	*Setup*	*Control Code*	*Decimal*	*Hexadecimal*
Wide print (5 cpi)	^N	(SO)	14	0E
Compressed print (17 cpi)	^O	(SI)	15	0F
Normal print (10 cpi)	^T	(DC4)	20	14

Formulas: The "formulas:" selection allows you to print formulas instead of values. To print formulas, simply **Tab** to the "formulas:" selection, type **Y** for Yes, and press **Return**. When this option is selected, the worksheet is often distorted, because formulas are most often wider than the values they represent. See the second sample session in Module 2 for an example of a formula display.

Row-Col Numbers The "row-col numbers:" selection allows you to print row and column numbers with your worksheet. To print row and column numbers, simply **Tab** to the "row-col numbers:" selection, type **Y** for Yes, and press **Return**.

APPLICATIONS

The Print commands are used to print your worksheets to your printer or to another file. Printing to a file lets you merge your worksheet with a word processed document. Once it has been displayed by a word processor, the worksheet can be modified to suit your needs.

The ability to adjust margins, print width, and print length is essential to print selected portions of a large worksheet. Often, portions of a worksheet are used as a "scratch pad." You'll want to prevent this area from printing by omitting it from the selected print area.

Printing formulas and column numbers is important if you want to pass a worksheet setup (sometimes called a *template*) to someone else in hardcopy form. You can also use this type of output for debugging purposes.

The "Setup:" selection is extremely important. Many users select compressed print in order to squeeze 132 characters into a standard 8 ½-inch page width.

TYPICAL OPERATION

In this illustration the Print command is used to adjust margins and worksheet size and finally to print the worksheet to a file. Remember, printing to a file is just like printing to a printer, except that the worksheet is transferred to a disk file instead of to the printer. Begin with Multiplan in the logged disk drive, and load the GPM.MP worksheet saved in Module 5.

1. Type **MP GPM.MP** and press **Return** to display the GPM.MP worksheet. (If you saved GPM.MP on the diskette in drive B, use B:GPM.MP.) Notice the following display.

```
                  1            2         3         4         5         6
 1                      Product Income and Cost Analysis
 2 ----------------------------------------------------------------------
 3 Item                     1 Qtr     2 Qtr     3 Qtr     4 Qtr     Total
 4 ======================================================================
 5 Sales               $11500.00 $13225.00 $15208.75 $17490.06 $57423.81
 6 Labor                $5620.00  $6322.50  $7112.81  $8001.91 $27057.23
 7 Material             $2445.00  $2811.75  $3233.51  $3718.54 $12208.80
 8 Total Cost           $8065.00  $9134.25 $10346.33 $11720.45 $39266.03
 9 ======================================================================
10 Gross Profit Margin  $3435.00  $4090.75  $4862.43  $5769.61 $18157.78
11 Cumulative GPM       $3435.00  $7525.75 $12388.18 $18157.78
12
13 GPM as a % of Sales      29.87%    30.93%    31.97%    32.99%    31.62%
14 ----------------------------------------------------------------------
```

2. Print the worksheet to a disk file, with the filename GPM.TXT. Proceed as follows:

   a. Start the Print Margins command and set the left margin to 5 (the default value), the top margin to 6 (default value), the print width to 80, the print length to 15, and the page length to 66 (default value) using the following keystrokes:

Keystrokes	*Results*				
P	PRINT: Printer File Margins Options				
M	PRINT MARGINS:	left: 5	top: 6	print width: 70	print length: 66
Tab Tab 80	PRINT MARGINS:	left: 5	top: 6	print width: 80	print length: 66
Tab 15	PRINT MARGINS:	left: 5	top: 6	print width: 80	print length: 15
Tab		page length: 66			
Return	PRINT: Printer File Margins Options				

   b. Start the Print Options command and set the print area to R1:15, the setup for compressed print (although this has no effect on file printing), formulas to No (the default value), and row-col numbers to Yes using the following keystrokes:

Keystrokes	*Results*		
O	PRINT OPTIONS:	area: R1:4095	setup:
R1:15	PRINT OPTIONS:	area: R1:15	setup:
Tab ^O	PRINT OPTIONS:	area: R1:15	setup: ^O
Tab Tab Y		formulas: Yes(No)	row-col numbers:(Yes)No
Return	PRINT: Printer File Margins Options		

   c. Start the Print File command, naming the worksheet GPM.TXT and using the following keystrokes (use B:GPM.TXT to write the file to the diskette in drive B.)

Keystrokes	*Results*
F	PRINT on file:
GPM.TXT	PRINT on file: GPM.TXT
Return	Completes Print File command

3. Notice that once the file is printed to disk, the main command line is redisplayed.
4. Quit by typing **Q Y** for Quit Yes; the operating system prompt is displayed.
5. From the system (or DOS) prompt, type **TYPE GPM.TXT** (use B:GPM.TXT if you wrote the file to drive B) to view the GPM.TXT file on your screen.

Module 21
QUIT

DESCRIPTION

The Quit command is used to exit Multiplan and return to the operating system prompt. Before quitting, you should be sure to save your worksheet using the Transfer Save command. Once the worksheet is saved, type **Q** to Quit.

If you have made changes to the displayed worksheet, Multiplan gives you the opportunity to save the edits, discard (or lose) them, or to cancel the Quit operation. The following information is displayed when you use Quit after editing a worksheet.

```
QUIT:

Enter Y to save edits, N to lose edits, or cancel
RnCn          Cell Contents          99% Free     Multiplan: FILENAME
```

Type **Y** to save the current worksheet as edited, and the operating system prompt is displayed. If you change your mind, you can type **N** to lose the edits, or press **Esc** if you decide not to quit. Pressing **Esc** redisplays the command line and you can continue working with your worksheet.

APPLICATIONS

The Quit command is used each time you want to end a Multiplan session. The "Enter Y to save . . ." message makes you think twice before you leave the current worksheet. It's a reminder to keep you from quitting before you've saved your worksheet. Of course, if you're only using a temporary worksheet or performing a temporary "what if" operation, you may want to lose any edits prior to quitting.

TYPICAL OPERATION

In this illustration the Quit command is used to leave a blank worksheet. Begin with Multiplan in the logged disk drive.

1. Type **MP** and press **Return** to display a blank worksheet.
2. Press **Return** to select Alpha, type **Name** in cell R1C1, and press **Return**.
3. Type **Q** for Quit and notice the following display.

```
             1          2       3       4       5       6
    1
    2
    3
    4
    5
    6
    7
    8
    9
   10
   11
   12
   13
   14
   15
   16
   17
   18
   19
   20
QUIT:

Enter Y to save edits, N to lose edits, or cancel
R1C1                        100% Free    Multiplan: TEMP
```

4. Type **N** to lose edits; notice that the operating system prompt is displayed.

Module 22

SORT

DESCRIPTION

The Sort command is used to arrange information within columns in alphabetical, numerical, or alphanumerical order. The information can be arranged in either ascending (>) or descending (<) order, where the > and < symbols are selected during the command process. The sorting sequence, in ascending (low-to-high) order is

! " # $ & ' ( ) * + , – . / 0-9 : ; < + > ? @ A-Z [\ ] _ ' a-z { : } ~

Sorting collects different types of characters into groups, which are

- Numbers
- Text
- Logical and error values
- Blank cells

If two identical values are encountered during a sort, they are left in their original order.

The form of the Sort command is

```
SORT by column: 1     between rows: 1     and: 4095    order:(>)<

Enter a number
R1C1        Cell Contents          99% Free     Multiplan: FILENAME
```

MULTIPLE SORTS Multiple sorts can be used by sorting the least significant column first, and then sorting each subsequent column in order of importance until the most significant column is sorted. For example, if you're sorting states, counties, and cities, the sorting order would be cities first, then counties, and finally states. This places all cities in alphabetical order within counties. Likewise, counties are arranged in alphabetical order within states. Finally, the third sort arranges states in alphabetical order.

SORT ILLUSTRATION To illustrate use of the sort command, a personnel roster containing employee names and department numbers is used. The roster is shown in the following worksheet.

```
                1             2         3
 1      Personnel Employment Roster
 2 ====================================
 3 Employee Name       Dept. No.
 4 ====================================
 5 Davis, George T.         1300
 6 Thompson, Bill O.        1200
 7 Janson, Marie G.         1000
 8 Tipton, Walter A.        1300
 9 Jones, Janice R.         1200
10 Phillips, Walter P.      1000
11 Stine, Frank N.          1300
12 Counts, Benjamin D.      1100
13 Russell, Allen S.        1000
14 Dickson, Carol A.        1200
15 Zumr, Margaret A.        1100
16 Colley, Susan T.         1200
```

To sort the Personnel Employment Roster by name within department, two sorts are required. Begin by positioning the cell pointer to R5C1 and typing

Keystrokes	*Results*			
S	SORT by column: 1	between rows: 1	and: 4095	order:(>)<
TAB 5	SORT by column: 1	between rows: 5	and: 4095	order:(>)<
Return	Completes first Sort command			

The result of this sort rearranges the worksheet in the following way:

```
               1             2          3
  1     Personnel Employment Roster
  2 ===================================
  3 Employee Name        Dept. No.
  4 ===================================
  5 Colley, Susan T.          1200
  6 Counts, Benjamin D.       1100
  7 Davis, George T.          1300
  8 Dickson, Carol A.         1200
  9 Janson, Marie G.          1000
 10 Jones, Janice R.          1200
 11 Phillips, Walter P.       1000
 12 Russell, Allen S.         1000
 13 Stine, Frank N.           1300
 14 Thompson, Bill O.         1200
 15 Tipton, Walter A.         1300
 16 Zumr, Margaret A.         1100
```

Next, the "Dept. No." column is sorted by positioning the cell pointer to R5C2 and typing

Keystrokes	*Results*
S	SORT by column: 2 between rows: 5 and: 4095 order:(>)<
Return	Completes second Sort command

Notice that the "between rows:" selection "remembered" the previous sort setup. The second sort rearranges the worksheet in the following way:

```
               1             2          3
  1     Personnel Employment Roster
  2 ===================================
  3 Employee Name        Dept. No.
  4 ===================================
  5 Janson, Marie G.          1000
  6 Phillips, Walter P.       1000
  7 Russell, Allen S.         1000
  8 Counts, Benjamin D.       1100
  9 Zumr, Margaret A.         1100
 10 Colley, Susan T.          1200
 11 Dickson, Carol A.         1200
 12 Jones, Janice R.          1200
 13 Thompson, Bill O.         1200
 14 Davis, George T.          1300
 15 Stine, Frank N.           1300
 16 Tipton, Walter A.         1300
```

Notice that employee names are arranged in alphabetical order within departments.

APPLICATIONS

The Sort command is used to arrange items such as ZIP codes, dates, and names in alphabetical or numerical order. If you are sorting on dates, where the year is significant, you may want to enter your dates in the form YY/MM/DD, where YY = year, MM = month, and DD = day. An alternative is to place the year in a separate column and use a multiple sort to first arrange the month and day, and then the year.

Using conventional MM/DD/YY notation does not have the desired effect when sorting. For instance, the dates 01/05/86, 01/10/84, and 10/21/81 are sorted

```
01/05/86
01/10/84
10/21/81
```

Some Multiplan users maintain telephone directories in their worksheet. As new names and numbers are added, the Sort command is used to arrange the names in alphabetical order. An example of a telephone directory worksheet is shown in the Typical Operation section of this module.

TYPICAL OPERATION

In this illustration a Telephone Directory worksheet is constructed and the Sort command is used to alphabetize the names. Begin with Multiplan in the logged disk drive.

1. Type **MP** and press **Return** to display a blank worksheet.
2. Use the Format Default Cells command to place the worksheet in the continuous (Cont) text entry mode (see Module 10).
3. Use the Format Width command to adjust the width of column 1 to 20 characters and column 2 to 14 characters.
4. Type the title **Telephone Directory** using the Alpha command; start the title with 8 blank spaces.
5. Use the Alpha command to construct the following worksheet.

```
                 1                 2
   1           Telephone Directory
   2           Name              Number
   3 ===================================
   4
   5
   6
   7
   8
```

6. Use the Alpha command to enter the names and numbers contained in the following worksheet.

```
               1                  2
1         Telephone Directory
2         Name               Number
3 ===================================
4 Johnson, Albert      (512) 259-9890
5 Jackson, Donald      (303) 545-8785
6 Ackard, John         (214) 423-0907
7 Dillon, Cecil        (201) 593-3606
8 Tildon, William      (208) 565-2720
```

7. Position the cell pointer to R4C1 and type

Keystrokes	*Results*			
S	SORT by column: 1	between rows: 1	and: 4095	order:(>)<
TAB 4	SORT by column: 1	between rows: 4	and: 4095	order:(>)<
Return	Completes first Sort command			

8. Notice that the rows have been rearranged so that the names are in alphabetical order.

```
               1                  2
1         Telephone Directory
2         Name               Number
3 ===================================
4 Ackard, John         (214) 423-0907
5 Dillon, Cecil        (201) 593-3606
6 Jackson, Donald      (303) 545-8785
7 Johnson, Albert      (512) 259-9890
8 Tildon, William      (208) 565-2720
```

9. Save the Telephone directory for personal use by typing **T S PHONE.TXT** and pressing **Return**.
10. Quit by typing **Q**; the operating system prompt is displayed.

Module 23

TRANSFER

DESCRIPTION

The Transfer command is used to control file operations, including loading, saving, renaming, and deleting files. The Transfer Options form of the command lets you choose which disk drive to use. It also is used to control the file format of loaded and saved files, enabling Multiplan to be used with files generated by other programs. Finally, the Transfer Clear command is used to clear the active worksheet.

A useful feature of the Transfer command is the ability to view a file directory. Once the Transfer Load or Transfer Delete commands are active, you can press a cursor key to view a disk directory. When the directory is displayed, you can select a file for loading or deleting by moving to the filename with your cursor control keys and pressing **Return**.

The form of the Transfer command is

```
TRANSFER: Load Save Clear Delete Options Rename

Select option or type command letter
RnCn        Cell Contents          99% Free     Multiplan: FILENAME
```

The following six paragraphs within this section describe the various forms of the Transfer command.

CLEAR The Transfer Clear command is used to clear the worksheet in preparation for creating a new worksheet or loading an existing one. To clear your worksheet, type

Keystrokes	*Results*
T	TRANSFER: Load Save Clear Delete Options Rename
C	Enter Y to confirm
Y	Completes Transfer Clear command

LOAD The Transfer Load command is used to load an existing worksheet from disk into a clear worksheet display. The form of this command is

```
TRANSFER LOAD filename:

Enter a filename, or use direction keys to view directory
RnCn        Cell Contents         99% Free     Multiplan: FILENAME
```

To load a worksheet file with the filename ANALYSIS.MP, type

Keystrokes	*Results*
T	TRANSFER: Load Save Clear Delete Options Rename
L	TRANSFER LOAD filename:
ANALYSIS.MP	TRANSFER LOAD filename: ANALYSIS.MP
Return	Completes Transfer Load command.

An alternative to typing the filename in the above sequence is to press a cursor key once the "TRANSFER LOAD filename" is displayed. This displays the disk file directory. Move to the desired filename with the cursor key and press **Return** to load the file.

Transferring Other Worksheets into Multiplan You can load Lotus 1-2-3, Lotus Symphony, and VisiCalc worksheets directly into Multiplan. dBASEII and columnar text files can also be loaded into Multiplan using the CONVERTD utility supplied with Multiplan 2.0. This utility is self prompting. Just type **CONVERTD** and press **Return**. The prompts and menus guide you through the process.

Loading a Lotus 1-2-3 Worksheet To load a Lotus 1-2-3 worksheet directly into Multiplan, first set the Transfer Options command to "(Other)." To familiarize you with this process, the procedure for transferring a Lotus 1-2-3 worksheet into Multiplan follows.

Look at the following Lotus 1-2-3 sample worksheet.

A1: 'Part

	A	B	C	D	E	F	G	H
1	Part	-----Unit-----		Number	-----Total-----		Margin	Margin
2	Number	Cost	Price	Sold	Cost	Price	Dollars	Percent
3	--------	--------	--------	--------	--------	--------	--------	--------
4	A-09-87-F	$1.29	$1.68	123	$158.67	$206.27	$47.60	30.00%
5	A-09-88-M	$3.33	$4.33	123	$409.59	$532.47	$122.88	30.00%
6	B-23-96-X	$2.24	$2.91	50	$112.00	$145.60	$33.60	30.00%
7	D-05-01-X	$1.02	$1.33	24	$24.48	$31.82	$7.34	30.00%
8	G-18-22-F	$1.88	$2.44	64	$120.32	$156.42	$36.10	30.00%
9	G-18-22-M	$1.95	$2.54	64	$124.80	$162.24	$37.44	30.00%
10	--------	--------	--------	--------	--------	--------	--------	--------
11	Total/Avg	$1.95	$2.54	448	$949.86	$1,234.82	$284.96	30.00%

The name of the Lotus 1-2-3 worksheet is SALES.WKS. The following cells contain the indicated text strings and Lotus 1-2-3 formulas. The cells in rows 3 and 10 contain \-, which is a continuous hyphen (or rule). The remainder of the cells contain the indicated values.

B1: ' - - - - -Unit- - - - -
E1: ' - - - - -Total- - - - -
B11: @AVG(B9. .B4)
C11: @AVG(C9. .C4)
D11: @SUM(D9. .D4)
E11: @SUM(E9. .E4)
F11: @SUM(F9. .F4)
G11: @SUM(G9. .G4)
H11: @AVG(H9. .H4)

Notice that the text in cell B1 continues into cell C1. The text in E1 continues into F1. Cells B11 through H11 contain Lotus 1-2-3 average and summation formulas.

Lotus 1-2-3 macros are transferred as text. Some Lotus 1-2-3 functions are deleted by Multiplan, but values within the formula cells are retained. These are:

@ACOS	@DAY	@DVAR
@ASIN	@DCOUNT	@HLOOKUP
@ATAN2	@DMAX	@MONTH
@CHOOSE	@DMIN	@RAND
@DATE	@DSTD	@VAR
@DAVG	@DSUM	@YEAR

To Transfer Load the Lotus 1-2-3 worksheet SALES.WKS, proceed as follows:

1. Type **T O** for Transfer Options and notice the following display.

```
TRANSFER OPTIONS mode:(Normal)Symbolic Other    setup:

Enter text
```

2. Select Other by pressing the **Spacebar** twice. Then press **Return**

```
TRANSFER OPTIONS mode: Normal Symbolic(Other)   setup:

Enter text
```

3. Now type **T L** for Transfer Load; enter the worksheet name **SALES.WKS** and press **Return**.

```
TRANSFER LOAD filename: SALES.WKS

Enter filename or use direction keys to select from list
```

4. The SALES.WKS file loads and your display resembles the following screen illustration.

#1	1	2	3	4	5	6	7	8
1	Part	-----U		Number	-----Tot		Margin	Margin
2	Number	Cost	Price	Sold	Cost	Price	Dollars	Percent
3	----------------	----------	----------	----------	----------	----------	----------	----------
4	A-09-87-F	$1.29	$1.68	123	$158.67	$206.27	$47.60	30.00%
5	A-09-88-M	$3.33	$4.33	123	$409.59	$532.47	$122.88	30.00%
6	B-23-96-X	$2.24	$2.91	50	$112.00	$145.60	$33.60	30.00%
7	D-05-01-X	$1.02	$1.33	24	$24.48	$31.82	$7.34	30.00%
8	G-18-22-F	$1.88	$2.44	64	$120.32	$156.42	$36.10	30.00%
9	G-18-22-M	$1.95	$2.54	64	$124.80	$162.24	$37.44	30.00%
10	----------------	----------	----------	----------	----------	----------	----------	----------
11	Total/Avg	$1.95	$2.54	448	$949.86	$1234.82	$284.96	30.00%

5. Adjust the continuous text strings using the Format Cells Cont command.
6. Check you AVERAGE and SUM formulas; notice that they are in Multiplan format.
7. Save the worksheet as a Multiplan binary file by resetting Transfer Option back to Normal. When the worksheet file is saved, it is reconfigured to the Multiplan binary file format. This format takes less disk space and loads faster.

Saving a Multiplan worksheet in Lotus 1-2-3 Format You can also save a 1-2-3 Worksheet as a Lotus 1-2-3 worksheet file by using the Transfer Options Other setup and giving the worksheet name a .WKS extension. Multiplan macros are not translated by 1-2-3. However, they become usable again if you load them back into Multiplan.

Some Multiplan functions are not interpreted by Lotus 1-2-3. The cell contents are transferred as values. These are:

COLUMN	LEN	REPT
DELTA	LOOKUP	ROUND
DOLLAR	MID	ROW
FIXED	MIRR	SIGN
INDEX	NPER	VALUE
ITERCNT	RATE	

SAVE The Transfer Save command is used to save the displayed worksheet to disk. The form of this command is

```
TRANSFER SAVE filename:

Enter filename or use direction keys to select from list
RnCn          Cell Contents          99% Free     Multiplan: FILENAME
```

To save a worksheet with the filename ANALYSIS.MP, type

Keystrokes	*Results*
T	TRANSFER: Load Save Clear Delete Options Rename
S	TRANSFER SAVE filename:
ANALYSIS.MP	TRANSFER SAVE filename: ANALYSIS.MP
Return	Completes Transfer Save command.

If the file ANALYSIS.MP already exists, Multiplan asks, "Overwrite existing file?" Typing **Y** for Yes writes the active worksheet over the old one. Typing **N** for No cancels the Transfer Save command.

RENAME The Transfer Rename command is used to rename an active worksheet before it is filed. It also adjusts links to supporting and dependent worksheets (see Xternal command, Module 26). Finally, the Transfer Rename command deletes the old worksheet file containing the previous name. The form of this command is

```
TRANSFER RENAME filename:

Enter a filename
RnCn          Cell Contents          99% Free     Multiplan: FILENAME
```

To rename an active worksheet with the filename ANALYSIS.MP, type

Keystrokes	*Results*
T	TRANSFER: Load Save Clear Delete Options Rename
R	TRANSFER RENAME filename:
ANALYSIS.MP	TRANSFER RENAME filename: ANALYSIS.MP
Return	Overwrite existing file?
Y	Completes Transfer Rename command

DELETE The Transfer Delete command is used to delete a file from your diskette. The form of this command is

```
TRANSFER DELETE filename:

Enter a filename
RnCn        Cell Contents          99% Free     Multiplan: FILENAME
```

To delete a file with the filename OLDSTUFF, type

Keystrokes	*Results*
T	TRANSFER: Load Save Clear Delete Options Rename
D	TRANSFER DELETE filename:
OLDSTUFF	TRANSFER DELETE filename: OLDSTUFF
Return	Enter Y to confirm
Y	Completes Transfer Delete command

OPTIONS The Transfer Options command is used to control the file format "mode" used when files are loaded and saved with the Transfer Load and Transfer Save commands. It also offers a Transfer Options Setup command, which selects the default disk drive. The form of the Transfer Options command is

```
TRANSFER OPTIONS mode: Normal Symbolic Other     setup:

Select option
RnCn        Cell Contents          99% Free     Multiplan: FILENAME
```

Transfer Options Mode The Transfer Options Mode command lets you select the file type use in conjunction with loading and saving files. Selection of the Other mode is made by typing

Keystrokes	*Results*
T	TRANSFER: Load Save Clear Delete Options Rename
O	TRANSFER OPTIONS mode: Normal Symbolic Other
O	TRANSFER OPTIONS mode: Normal Symbolic(Other)
Return	Completes Transfer Options command

The Symbolic and Normal modes are similarly selected by typing the first letter of the option. A brief description of each of these modes is given in the following list.

Mode	*Description*
Normal	The Normal mode is simply standard Multiplan binary format. This format makes efficient use of disk space; it operates with Xternal Multiplan worksheets (see Module 26).
Symbolic	The Symbolic mode makes the worksheet file compatible with other programs that use symbolic link (SYLK) file format. SYLK files, which are encoded in ASCII, are divided into records by either a carriage return (0Dh) or line feed (0Ah) character. Empty records are ignored. SYLK files also contain record- and field-type descriptors. Record-type descriptors establish cell coordinates, values, protection states, computational expressions, and so on. Field-type descriptors determine the meaning of fields. These are described in your Multiplan documentation.
Other	The Other mode lets Multiplan load Lotus 1-2-3, Lotus Symphony, and VisiCalc worksheet files. Once loaded, you can set Transfer Options back to Normal and save the worksheet as a Multiplan file. If the Other mode is kept, the file is saved in its original format. See the Transfer Load command for the procedure used to load a Lotus 1-2-3 worksheet.

Transfer Options Setup The Transfer Options Setup command lets you change the default disk drive. For example, if you wish to specify disk drive B as the default drive, type

Keystrokes	*Results*	
T	TRANSFER: Load Save Clear Delete Options Rename	
O	TRANSFER OPTIONS mode: Normal Symbolic Other	setup:
Tab B:	TRANSFER OPTIONS mode:(Normal)Symbolic Other	setup: B:
Return	Completes Transfer Options command	

APPLICATIONS

The Transfer commands are used for loading and saving files. You can view your disk directory, delete unwanted files, change the name of your active worksheet, and change the file format to make your worksheet compatible with files either generated or used by other programs. You can also use the Transfer command to clear an unwanted worksheet. Finally, you can use the Transfer command to change the default disk drive during worksheet use. All these applications make the Transfer command one of the most heavily used commands.

TYPICAL OPERATION

In this illustration the Transfer command is used to load a worksheet and then to save it. Begin with Multiplan in the logged disk drive.

1. Type **MP** and press **Return** to display a blank worksheet.

2. Load the GPM.MP worksheet by typing

Keystrokes	*Results*
T	TRANSFER: Load Save Clear Delete Options Rename
L	TRANSFER LOAD filename:
GPM.MP	TRANSFER LOAD filename: GPM.MP
Return	Completes Transfer Load command.

3. Notice the following display after the worksheet loads.

```
                 1                2         3         4         5         6
 1                          Product Income and Cost Analysis
 2 ----------------------------------------------------------------------
 3 Item                         1 Qtr     2 Qtr     3 Qtr     4 Qtr     Total
 4 ======================================================================
 5 Sales                    $11500.00 $13225.00 $15208.75 $17490.06 $57423.81
 6 Labor                     $5620.00  $6322.50  $7112.81  $8001.91 $27057.23
 7 Material                  $2445.00  $2811.75  $3233.51  $3718.54 $12208.80
 8 Total Cost                $8065.00  $9134.25 $10346.33 $11720.45 $39266.03
 9 ======================================================================
10 Gross Profit Margin       $3435.00  $4090.75  $4862.43  $5769.61 $18157.78
11 Cumulative GPM            $3435.00  $7525.75 $12388.18 $18157.78
12
13 GPM as a % of Sales         29.87%    30.93%    31.97%    32.99%    31.62%
14 ----------------------------------------------------------------------
```

4. Save the worksheet using the Transfer Save command as follows:

Keystrokes	*Results*
T	TRANSFER: Load Save Clear Delete Options Rename
S	TRANSFER SAVE filename: GPM.MP
Return	Overwrite existing file?
Y	Completes Transfer Save command.

5. Quit by typing **Q**; the operating system prompt is displayed.

Module 24

VALUE

DESCRIPTION

The Value command is used to enter numbers and formulas into worksheet cells. Numbers can be entered and displayed as whole numbers, decimal fractions, dollars and cents, percentages, scientific notation, or a row of asterisks (*) for use in horizontal bar charts. For purposes of discussion, we'll use the term *value* to refer to either numbers or formulas.

STARTING THE VALUE COMMAND There are several ways to start the Value command. First, position the cell pointer to the cell in which you want to enter a value. Next, type **V** for Value, and you're ready to enter a formula or number. You can also highlight the Value command by pressing the **Tab** key or space bar until "Value" is highlighted on the command line. Then press **Return** to enter a number or formula. Still another way to start the Value command is to type 0 through 9, =, +, −, or (.

Finally, if you're entering text and numbers and using cursor keys to complete entries without pressing **Return**, typing a number or mathematical operator starts the Value command. Conversely, typing an alphabetical character starts the Alpha command. When a cursor key is used to complete a command, you'll notice "ALPHA/VALUE:" displayed on the entry line. This designates that either a number or sign or an alphabetical letter can be used to start either the Alpha or Value commands.

When **V** is pressed, the following information appears on your display screen.

```
VALUE:

Enter a formula
RnCn                                 99% Free     Multiplan: FILENAME
```

At this point you can type the value of your choice. If you make a typographical error, you can use the **Back Space** key to back up. If you want to move to the beginning of the value without "rubbing out" the preceding characters, use the **F9** key to move the cursor left. Use **F10** to move the cursor right on the entry line. Once the cursor is positioned, characters are automatically inserted. To delete one or more characters, use the **Del** key. Remember, the cursor keys control the cell pointer, not the entry cursor. Once a value is entered, press **Return** and the result appears in the cell.

Also notice that the value within the designated cell appears on the bottom line of the screen. You can verify if the entry is a number or formula. If the value is longer than ten characters, which is the default cell width, you'll have to reformat the column width to match the length of the longest value in that column. The method used to change column widths is described in Module 10.

FORMULAS Formulas contain cell references, mathematical and logical operators, and sometimes numbers. As you may recall from Module 2, cell references are in either absolute or relative notation. Absolute notation is the row and column number. This never changes relative to the position of the formula. Relative notation designates a cell position relative to the cell containing the formula. For example, if a value is used in a cell two rows up and one to the left of the current cell, the relative location is -2 rows, -1 column. Multiplan uses "R[-2]C[-1]" to express this relationship. If the formula is copied to another cell, the relative cell notation still relates to the position of the formula. Some examples of formulas are shown in Table 24-1.

Table 24-1 Formula Examples

Formula	*Description*
R1C3*25%	The value in cell R1C3 multiplied by 25 percent (.25).
R[-3]C	The value in the cell three rows above in the same column is displayed in the cell containing this relative cell expression.
SUM(R[-12]C:R[-2]C)	The sum of the value of all numbers in this column beginning 12 rows above and ending 2 rows above.
SUM(R[-2]C,RC[-1])	The sum of the value in the cell two rows above and the cell one column to the left.
R[-2]C + RC[-1]	The value in the cell two rows above added to the cell one column to the left.
1.05*(SUM(R2C2:R14C2))	The sum of all cells between R2C2 and R14C2 multiplied by 1.05.
AVERAGE(R3C3:R15C3)	The average of the values in the cells between R3C3 and R15C3.
IF((R15C5 = R15C10), "In Balance", "Out of Balance")	If the value in cell R15C5 is equal to the value in cell R15C10, "In Balance" is displayed; otherwise, "Out of Balance" is displayed.

APPLICATIONS

The Value and Alpha commands are the most frequently used commands in Multiplan. All worksheets used to compute values use formulas. As shown in Table 24-1, formulas are made up of numbers, mathematical and logical operators, and cell references. Cell references, which are in either absolute or relative notation as described in Module 2, use the numeric value within the referenced cell.

TYPICAL OPERATION

In this illustration the Value command is used to enter formulas and numbers in the GPM.MP worksheet prepared in Module 5. We'll begin by starting Multiplan and simultaneously loading the GPM.MP worksheet created and saved in Module 5. Start with Multiplan in logged disk disk drive.

1. Type **MP GPM.MP** and press **Return** to display the GPM.MP worksheet. If you saved GPM.MP on the diskette in drive B, use B:GPM.MP.
2. Notice that the following worksheet is displayed.

```
                      1              2          3          4          5          6
 1                         Product Income and Cost Analysis
 2 ----------------------------------------------------------------------
 3 Item                    1 Qtr      2 Qtr      3 Qtr      4 Qtr      Total
 4 ======================================================================
 5 Sales
 6 Labor
 7 Material
 8 Total Cost
 9 ======================================================================
10 Gross Profit Margin
11 Cumulative GPM
12
13 GPM as a % of Sales
15 ----------------------------------------------------------------------
```

3. Add labor and material and put the result in row 8 as follows:
   a. Position the cell pointer to cell R8C2 and enter the following keystrokes.

Keystrokes	*Results*
V	VALUE:
Cell pointer to R6C2	VALUE: R[-2]C
+	VALUE: R[-2]C+
Cell pointer to R5C2	VALUE: R[-2]C+R[-1]
Return	Completes formula entry

b. Copy the formula right four cells by entering the following keystrokes.

Keystrokes	*Results*
C R 4	COPY RIGHT 4 Cells
Return	Completes copy

4. Compute the gross profit margin by subtracting total cost from sales and put the result in row 10 as follows:

a. Position the cell pointer to R10C2 and enter the following keystrokes.

Keystrokes	*Results*
V	VALUE:
Cell pointer to R5C2	VALUE: R[-5]C
–	VALUE: R[-5]C-
Cell pointer to R8C2	VALUE: R[-5]C-R[-2]C
Return	Completes formula entry

b. Copy the formula right four cells by entering the following keystrokes.

Keystrokes	*Results*
C R 4	COPY RIGHT 4 Cells
Return	Completes copy

5. Compute the first quarter's cumulative gross profit margin (GPM) by positioning the cell pointer to R11C2 and entering the following keystrokes.

Keystrokes	*Results*
V	VALUE:
Cell pointer to R10C2	VALUE: R[-1]C
Return	Completes entry

6. Compute the cumulative GPM by adding the second quarter's profit margin to the first quarter's cumulative value as follows:

a. Position the cell pointer to R11C3 and enter the following keystrokes.

Keystrokes	*Results*
V	VALUE:
Cell pointer to R10C3	VALUE: R[-1]C
+	VALUE: R[-1]C+
Left Arrow to R11C2	VALUE: R[-1]C+RC[-1]
Return	Completes entry

b. Copy the formula right two cells by entering the following keystrokes.

Keystrokes	*Results*
C R 2	COPY RIGHT 2 Cells
Return	Completes copy

7. Calculate the gross profit margin as a percentage of sales as follows:

   a. Position the cell pointer to R13C2 and enter the following keystrokes.

Keystrokes	*Results*
V	VALUE:
Cell pointer to R10C2	VALUE: R[-3]C
/	VALUE: R[-3]C/
Cell pointer to R5C2	VALUE: R[-3]C/R[-8]C
Return	Completes entry (#DIV/0! displayed)

   b. Copy the formula right four cells by entering the following keystrokes.

Keystrokes	*Results*
C R 4	COPY RIGHT 4 Cells
Return	Completes copy

8. Add rows 5, 6, 7, and 8 and place the results in the "Total" column (C6) as follows:

   a. Position the cell pointer to R5C6 and enter the following keystrokes.

Keystrokes	*Results*
V	VALUE:
SUM(	VALUE: SUM(
Cell pointer to R5C2	VALUE: SUM(RC[-4]
:	VALUE: SUM(RC[-4]:
Cell pointer to R5C5	VALUE: SUM(RC[-4]:RC[-1]
)	VALUE: SUM(RC[-4]:RC[-1])
Return	Completes entry

   b. Copy the formula down three cells by entering the following keystrokes.

Keystrokes	*Results*
C D 3	COPY DOWN 3 Cells
Return	Completes copy

9. Assuming a 15 percent quarterly growth in sales, enter a formula that increases the first-quarter sales figure by 15 percent as follows:

   a. Position the cell pointer to R5C3 and enter the following keystrokes.

Keystrokes	*Results*
V	VALUE:
1.15*	VALUE: 1.15*
Cell pointer to R5C2	VALUE: 1.15*RC[-1]
Return	Completes entry

   b. Copy the formula right two cells by entering the following keystrokes.

Keystrokes	*Results*
C R 2	COPY RIGHT 2 Cells
Return	Completes copy

10. Assuming a 12.5 percent quarterly increase in labor cost, enter a formula that increases the first-quarter labor cost by 12.5 percent as follows:

    a. Position the cell pointer to R6C3 and enter the following keystrokes.

Keystrokes	*Results*
V	VALUE:
1.125*	VALUE: 1.125*
Cell pointer to R6C2	VALUE: 1.125*RC[-1]
Return	Completes formula entry

    b. Copy the formula right two cells by entering the following keystrokes.

Keystrokes	*Results*
C R 2	COPY RIGHT 2 Cells
Return	Completes Copy Right command

11. Assuming that material cost grows in proportion to sales, enter a formula that increases material cost by 15 percent by copying the formula from cell R5C3 and then copying it right two cells.

    a. Position the cell pointer to R7C3.

    b. Enter the following keystrokes.

Keystrokes	*Results*
C F	COPY FROM:
Cell pointer to R5C3	COPY FROM: R[-2]C
Return	Completes Copy From command
C R 2	COPY RIGHT 2 Cells
Return	Completes Copy Right command

12. Enter sales and cost information as shown in the following example.

```
               1              2         3         4         5         6
 1                            Product Income and Cost Analysis
 2 ----------------------------------------------------------------------
 3 Item                   1 Qtr     2 Qtr     3 Qtr     4 Qtr     Total
 4 ======================================================================
 5 Sales                     11500     13225  15208.75 17490.063 57423.813
 6 Labor                      5620    6322.5 7112.8125 8001.9141 27057.227
 7 Material                   2445   2811.75 3233.5125 3718.5394 12208.802
 8 Total Cost                 8065   9134.25 10346.325 11720.453 39266.028
 9 ======================================================================
10 Gross Profit Margin        3435   4090.75  4862.425 5769.6091 18157.784
11 Cumulative GPM             3435   7525.75 12388.175 18157.784
12
13 GPM as a % of Sales 0.2986957 0.3093195 0.3197123 0.3298793 0.3162065
14 ----------------------------------------------------------------------
```

By using the Format command, you can display dollars and cents notation to improve the appearance of the worksheet. This process is described in Module 10. The worksheet is shown with formulas instead of values in the following illustration.

```
                               1          2               3               4               5               6
 1                     "Product Income and Cost Analysis"
 2 "--------------------" "----------" "----------" "----------" "----------" "----------"
 3 "Item"                 "1 Qtr"        "2 Qtr"         "3 Qtr"         "4 Qtr"         "Total"
 4 "====================" "==========" "==========" "==========" "==========" "=========="
 5 "Sales"                11500          RC[-1]*1.15     RC[-1]*1.15     RC[-1]*1.15     SUM(RC[-4]:RC[-1])
 6 "Labor"                5620           1.125*RC[-1]    1.125*RC[-1]    1.125*RC[-1]    SUM(RC[-4]:RC[-1])
 7 "Material"             2445           RC[-1]*1.15     RC[-1]*1.15     RC[-1]*1.15     SUM(RC[-4]:RC[-1])
 8 "Total Cost"           R[-2]C+R[-1]C  R[-2]C+R[-1]C   R[-2]C+R[-1]C   R[-2]C+R[-1]C   SUM(RC[-4]:RC[-1])
 9 "====================" "==========" "==========" "==========" "==========" "=========="
10 "Gross Profit Margin"  R[-5]C-R[-2]C  R[-5]C-R[-2]C   R[-5]C-R[-2]C   R[-5]C-R[-2]C   R[-5]C-R[-2]C
11 "Cumulative GPM"       R[-1]C         R[-1]C+RC[-1]   R[-1]C+RC[-1]   R[-1]C+RC[-1]
12
13 "GPM as a % of Sales"  R[-3]C/R[-8]C  R[-3]C/R[-8]C   R[-3]C/R[-8]C   R[-3]C/R[-8]C   R[-3]C/R[-8]C
14 "--------------------" "----------" "----------" "----------" "----------" "----------"
```

13. Save your worksheet for later use by typing **T S** for Transfer Save and **Y** for overwrite; then press **Return**.
14. Quit Multiplan by typing **Q**.

Module 25
WINDOW

DESCRIPTION

The Window command is used to separate a worksheet into two or more separate areas, or "windows." The form of the Window command is

```
WINDOW: Split Border Close Link Paint

Select option or type command letter
RnCn     Cell Contents              99% Free      Multiplan: FILENAME
```

The Window Split command is used to create windows. The Window Close command "closes," or eliminates, window separation. The Window Link command is used to synchronize cell movement of adjacent windows. Finally, the Window Border command lets you draw a box around windows. These forms of the Window command are described in the following paragraphs.

SPLIT The Window Split command lets you create vertical or horizontal windows or separate the body of your worksheet for row and column titles. The form for the Window Split command is

```
WINDOW SPLIT: Horizontal Vertical Titles

Select option or type command letter
RnCn        Cell Contents           99% Free     Multiplan: FILENAME
```

The Window Horizontal command creates a horizontal window, with a horizontal row of column numbers separating the new window from the rest of the worksheet. The Window Vertical command creates a vertical window. The new vertical window is separated from the rest of the worksheet by a column of row numbers on the left-hand edge. The original worksheet window (#1) plus two vertical windows (#2 and #4) and one horizontal window (#3) are shown in the following example.

```
 #1         1          2          3 #2         4          5
   1                                1
   2                                2
   3                                3
   4             ORIGINAL           4             WINDOW #2
   5             WORKSHEET          5             (VERTICAL)
   6             WINDOW             6
   7                                7
   8                                8
   9                                9
 #3         1          2          3           4 #4          5
  10                                            10
  11                                            11
  12                                            12
  13             WINDOW #3                      13   WINDOW #4
  14             (HORIZONTAL)                   14   (VERTICAL)
  15                                            15
  16                                            16
```

To create a window as shown, position the cursor to cell R1C4 and type

Keystrokes	*Results*	
W	WINDOW: Split Border Close Link	
S	WINDOW SPLIT: Horizontal Vertical Titles	
V	WINDOW SPLIT VERTICAL at column: 4	linked: Yes(No)
Return	Completes Window 2	
Cell pointer to R10C1		
W	WINDOW: Split Border Close Link	
S	WINDOW SPLIT: Horizontal Vertical Titles	
H	WINDOW SPLIT HORIZONTAL at row: 10	linked: Yes(No)
Return	Completes Window 3	
Cell pointer to R10C5		
W	WINDOW: Split Border Close Link	
S	WINDOW SPLIT: Horizontal Vertical Titles	
V	WINDOW SPLIT VERTICAL at column: 4	linked: Yes(No)
Return	Completes Window 4	

Linked The original window and the next window can be linked by pressing **Tab** to move to the "linked:" selection and typing **Y** for Yes. This causes cells in the current window to scroll in unison with those in the previous window. The linking affects either horizontal or vertical scrolling, depending upon vertical or horizontal window creation.

Moving Between Windows To move to a specific window, use the Goto Window command (described in Module 11). For example, to jump your cursor to window 3, type **G W 3** for Goto Window 3 and press **Return**.

Row and Column Titles If you move the cell pointer to a high-numbered cell, such as R45C30, row and column titles scroll out of view. You can keep them on screen with the Window Split Titles command. The form of this command is

```
WINDOW SPLIT TITLES: # of rows: 2     # of columns: 1

Enter a number
RnCn         Cell Contents            99% Free     Multiplan: FILENAME
```

You can specify the number of rows and columns used with titles by entering the appropriate row and column numbers. The row and column numbers are automatically entered by positioning the cell pointer before issuing the Window Split Titles command. For example, if you want to split the titles at row 3 and column 2, position the cell pointer to R3C2 and type

Keystrokes	*Results*
W	WINDOW: Split Border Close Link
S	WINDOW SPLIT: Horizontal Vertical Titles
T	WINDOW SPLIT TITLES: # of rows: 2 # of columns: 1
Return	Completes Window Split Titles command

BORDER The Window Border command draws a border around the selected window. The form for the Window Border command is

```
WINDOW change border in window number: 1

Enter a number
RnCn         Cell Contents            99% Free     Multiplan: FILENAME
```

If a window is already bordered, you can eliminate the border with the same command. If you wish to draw a border around window 3, type

Keystrokes	*Results*
W	WINDOW: Split Border Close Link
B	WINDOW change border in window number: 1
3	WINDOW change border in window number: 3
Return	Completes Window Border command

CLOSE The Window Close command is used to eliminate a selected window. The form for this command is

```
WINDOW CLOSE window number: 1

Enter a number
RnCn          Cell Contents                 99% Free     Multiplan: FILENAME
```

If you wish to close window number 4, type

Keystrokes	*Results*
W	WINDOW: Split Border Close Link
C	WINDOW CLOSE window number: 1
4	WINDOW CLOSE window number: 4
Return	Completes Window Close command

LINK As you move the cell pointer around within a window, the cells within the window scroll independently unless they are linked. They can be linked as they are created, using the Window Split command and tabbing to the "linked:" selection as described above. Or you can link cells using the Window Link command. Only adjoining windows can be linked. An attempt to link two windows that are separated by one or more intermediate windows results in the message: "Cannot link those windows."

The form for the Window Link command is

```
WINDOW LINK window number: 1    with window number: 2    linked: Yes(No)

Enter a number
RnCn          Cell Contents                 99% Free     Multiplan: FILENAME
```

To link windows 2 and 3, type

Keystrokes	*Results*
W	WINDOW: Split Border Close Link
C	WINDOW LINK window number: 1
2	WINDOW LINK window number: 2
Tab	with window number: 2 linked: Yes(No)
3	with window number: 3 linked: Yes(No)
Tab Y	with window number: 3 linked:(Yes)No
Return	Completes Window Link command

You can also use the Window Link command to check the status of linked windows. The "linked:(Yes)No" display indicates that the selected windows are linked.

PAINT If you have a color monitor, you can use the Paint option to set the foreground, background, and border colors. The form of the Paint command is

```
WINDOW PAINT foreground: 7     background: 0     border: 7

Enter color number or use direction keys to select color
```

You can use the cursor keys to rotate the color number and the display. This eliminates the need for you to enter numbers on a trial and error basis until you get a color combination that is pleasing. Just switch colors with the cursor keys until you see a combination you like. Once set, press **Return** to save the settings.

APPLICATIONS

You can create several separate mathematical tables or financial models on a single worksheet. These areas may be related or unrelated. The Window command lets you separate these worksheets into independently displayed areas.

There are also times when you want to hold a certain cell or series of cells–like the "Total" row–on the screen while entering data in other parts of your worksheet. This lets you see the effect of data entry on the cells in the "Total" row. The Window command lets you hold one window of a worksheet on screen while moving around in another.

TYPICAL OPERATION

In this illustration the Window Split Titles command is used with the GPM.MP worksheet. Begin with the Multiplan diskette in the logged disk drive.

1. Type **MP GPM.MP** and press **Return** to display the GPM.MP worksheet. (If you saved GPM.MP on the diskette in drive B, use B:GPM.MP.) Notice the following display.

```
                1             2         3         4         5         6
 1                   Product Income and Cost Analysis
 2 ----------------------------------------------------------------------
 3 Item                  1 Qtr     2 Qtr     3 Qtr     4 Qtr      Total
 4 ======================================================================
 5 Sales              $11500.00 $13225.00 $15208.75 $17490.06 $57423.81
 6 Labor               $5620.00  $6322.50  $7112.81  $8001,91 $27057.23
 7 Material            $2445.00  $2811.75  $3233.51  $3718.54 $12208.80
 8 Total Cost          $8065.00  $9134.25 $10346.33 $11720.45 $39266.03
 9 ======================================================================
10 Gross Profit Margin $3435.00  $4090.75  $4862.43  $5769.61 $18157.78
11 Cumulative GPM      $3435.00  $7525.75 $12388.18 $18157.78
12
13 GPM as a % of Sales   29.87%    30.93%    31.97%    32.99%    31.62%
14 ----------------------------------------------------------------------
```

2. Position the cell pointer to cell R5C2 and type

Keystrokes	*Results*
W	WINDOW: Split Border Close Link
S	WINDOW SPLIT: Horizontal Vertical Titles
T	WINDOW SPLIT TITLES: # of rows: 4 # of columns: 1
Return	Completes Window Split Titles command

3. Notice that titles are separated into windows as shown in the following display.

```
#1                 1    #2          2          3          4          5          6
  1                        Product Income and Cost Analysis
  2 --------------------    ----------------------------------------------------
  3 Item                     1 Qtr      2 Qtr      3 Qtr      4 Qtr      Total
  4 ====================    ====================================================
#4                      #3
  5 Sales                 $11500.00 $13225.00 $15208.75 $17490.06 $57423.81
  6 Labor                  $5620.00  $6322.50  $7112.81  $8001.91 $27057.23
  7 Material               $2445.00  $2811.75  $3233.51  $3718.54 $12208.80
  8 Total Cost             $8065.00  $9134.25 $10346.33 $11720.45 $39266.03
  9 ====================    ====================================================
 10 Gross Profit Margin    $3435.00  $4090.75  $4862.43  $5769.61 $18157.78
 11 Cumulative GPM         $3435.00  $7525.75 $12388.18 $18157.78
 12
 13 GPM as a % of Sales       29.87%     30.93%     31.97%     32.99%     31.62%
 14 -------------------------------------------------------------------------
```

4. Move the cell pointer around within the window and notice the display.
5. Jump the cell pointer to window number 1 by typing **G W 1** for Goto Window 1 and press **Return**.
6. Quit without saving by typing **Q N**; the operating system prompt is displayed.

Module 26

XTERNAL (OR EXTERNAL)

DESCRIPTION

The External command is used to establish a functional relationship between two or more worksheets. When the relationships are established, the contents of one or more cells on one worksheet can be used by another worksheet. The form of the External command is

```
EXTERNAL: Copy List Total Use

Select option or type command letter
RnCn     Cell Contents                  99% Free      Multiplan: FILENAME
```

The External Copy, List, and Use commands are described in the following paragraphs.

COPY The External Copy command lets you copy values from one worksheet into blank cells of another. The form of the External Copy command is

```
EXTERNAL COPY from sheet:            name:
              to: RnCn               linked:(Yes)No
Enter a filename
RnCn     Cell Contents                  99% Free      Multiplan: FILENAME
```

To illustrate the use of the External Copy command, assume that you want to copy the value of a cell named "TOTAL" of COST.MP worksheet to blank cell R9C6 of the active worksheet. (The Name command is described in Module 18.) Move the cell pointer to R9C6 and type

Keystrokes	*Results*	
X	EXTERNAL: Copy List Use	
C	EXTERNAL COPY from sheet:	name:
COST.MP	EXTERNAL COPY from sheet: COST.MP	name:
Tab TOTAL	EXTERNAL COPY from sheet: COST.MP	name: TOTAL
Return	Completes External Copy command	

If a cell or group of cells in the From sheet is unnamed, you can refer to it by row and column number. An entire section of a worksheet can be copied using the External Copy command, as long as it can be described by name or cell location. The Typical Operation section of this module illustrates how several cells within a row are copied.

The "linked" selection is used to establish a permanent relationship between the active worksheet and supporting worksheets. If a link is established, the values are automatically copied from supporting worksheets each time the dependent worksheet is loaded.

LIST The External List command is used to display a list of the worksheets that support the active worksheet and those that are dependent upon it. The form of the External Copy command is

```
Sheets supporting FILENAME.MP

LABOR.MP
MATERIAL.MP
OVERHEAD.MP


Sheets depending on FILENAME.MP

PROFIT.MP
DIVIDEND.MP
```

If no sheets support or depend on the active worksheet, the message "No sheets support (or depend on) FILENAME" is displayed.

TOTAL The External Total command lets you combine all or a portion of another worksheet with the current worksheet. The combined ranges must have identical structure to ensure data compatibility. For example, a 12-month total line on the incoming worksheet must match a 12-month total line on the current worksheet to avoid a data mismatch.

The form of the External Total command is

```
EXTERNAL TOTAL from sheet:          name:
           starting at:                   operation: + - * /
Enter a filename
RnCn    Cell Contents                 99% Free     Multiplan: FILENAME
```

Using the External Total command:

1. Enter one or more worksheet names to be combined in the "from sheet" field. You can combine multiple worksheets by separating the file names with a comma. You can use a range of worksheet names by using something like LABOR1:LABOR4 to combine worksheets named LABOR1, LABOR2, LABOR3, and LABOR4.

Note that the worksheet names are carefully structured. Multiplan uses the last character of worksheet names to put them in the proper order. If you use extensions, be sure they are consistent, like LABOR.001, LABOR.002, and so on. You can press a cursor key to display existing worksheet names.

2. Tab to the "name" field and enter an absolute range of cells, like R1C1:R12C14, or use the assigned name for the range of cells. As with worksheet names, you can also use a cursor key to display existing names.
3. Next, tab to the "starting at" field to identify the upper left-hand cell position of the incoming range, such as R12C3.
4. Finally, you use the "operation" field to specify what you want done with the incoming data, i.e., add, subtract, multiply, or divide.

When combining worksheet data, Multiplan follows a few practical rules to ensure that data is combined in a logical manner. These are:

1. Incoming text is inserted into blank cells.
2. Incoming text is ignored by cells within the current worksheet containing text, values, or formulas.
3. Incoming values are ignored by cells within the current worksheet containing text or formulas.
4. Incoming values are added to or subtracted from blank cells and cells containing values.

USE The External Use command lets you change the dependent links from one supporting worksheet to another. The form for the External Use command is

```
EXTERNAL USE filename:                  instead of:

Enter a filename
RnCn      Cell Contents                  99% Free      Multiplan: FILENAME
```

To illustrate the External Use command, let's say that you want to use the 85COST worksheet instead of the 84COST worksheet to support your active worksheet. To make the change, type

Keystrokes	*Results*	
X	EXTERNAL: Copy List Use	
U	EXTERNAL USE filename:	instead of:
85COST.MP	EXTERNAL USE filename: 85COST.MP	instead of:
Tab 84COST.MP	EXTERNAL USE filename: 85COST.MP	instead of: 84COST.MP
Return	Completes External Use command	

ELIMINATING AN EXTERNAL LINKAGE It is possible to dissolve the connection between two worksheets by using the External Copy command as follows:

1. Type **X C** for External Copy. The name of the last worksheet copied is displayed as the "from sheet."
2. Press **Tab** and type the name of the group of cells you want to unlink.
3. Press **Tab** again so that the cursor follows the "to" prompt.
4. Now press **Del** and **Return** to eliminate the external linkage.

ELIMINATING A DEFINED NAME You can delete the name of a group of cells established with the External Copy command as follows:

1. Type **N** for Name; Multiplan displays the last name defined. You can rotate established names with the cursor keys or by typing a name in the "define name" field.
2. Check that the "to refer to" field is blank.
3. Press **Return** to delete the defined name.

APPLICATIONS

The External command is one of Multiplan's most powerful commands. It lets you organize your worksheets into a functional series and then consolidate them by linking them to a summary (or master) worksheet. A good application example is the 1040 income tax form used by the U.S. Internal Revenue Service. You can duplicate Form 1040 on a worksheet and link it to the supporting 1040 tax schedules. Once the worksheets are set up with labels, formulas, and external links, all that is necessary is numerical entry. Multiplan does the rest.

TYPICAL OPERATION

In this illustration the External command is used to link a LABOR.MP and MATERIAL.MP worksheet to the GPM.MP worksheet. First, create the LABOR.MP and MATERIAL.MP worksheets. Next, link them to the GPM.MP worksheet. Begin with the Multiplan diskette in the logged disk drive.

1. Type **MP** and press **Return** to display a blank worksheet.
2. Use the Alpha and Value commands to create the following worksheet. Use the formula SUM(RC[-4]:RC[-1]) in cell R5C6 by moving the cell pointer to R5C6 and typing

Keystrokes	*Results*
V	VALUE:
SUM(	VALUE: SUM(
Cell pointer to R5C2	VALUE: SUM(RC[-4]
:	VALUE: SUM(RC[-4]:
Cell pointer to R5C5	VALUE: SUM(RC[-4]:RC[-1]
)	VALUE: SUM(RC[-4]:RC[-1])
Return	Completes formula entry

```
        1        2        3        4        5        6
1                      Labor Costs
2 ============================================================
3             1 Qtr    2 Qtr    3 Qtr    4 Qtr    Total
4 ============================================================
5 Labor Cost $5600.00 $5900.00 $6200.00 $6400.00 $24100.00
6 ============================================================
7
```

3. Name cells R5C2 through R5C5 "Labor" by typing:

Keystrokes	*Results*
N	NAME: define name:
LABOR	NAME: define name: LABOR
Tab	to refer to: R5C2
:	to refer to: R5C2:
Cell pointer to R5C5	to refer to: R5C2:R5C5
Return	Completes Name command

4. Save the worksheet by typing **T S LABOR.MP** and pressing **Return**.
5. Create a worksheet named MATERIAL.MP by editing the LABOR.MP worksheet to look like the following illustration. Use the Edit command to change the worksheet title and row headings. Use the Value command to enter new numbers. Use the Name command to rename cells R5C2 through R5C5 "Material." The formula in R5C6 is still valid.

```
        1        2        3        4        5        6
1                     Material Costs
2 ============================================================
3             1 Qtr    2 Qtr    3 Qtr    4 Qtr    Total
4 ============================================================
5 Mat'l Cost $2200.00 $2300.00 $2400.00 $2550.00 $9450.00
6 ============================================================
7
```

6. Save the worksheet by typing **T S MATERIAL.MP** and pressing **Return.**

7. Use the Transfer Load command to load the GPM.MP worksheet. Notice that the following worksheet is displayed.

```
                1           2         3         4         5         6
 1                      Product Income and Cost Analysis
 2 -------------------------------------------------------------------------
 3 Item                  1 Qtr     2 Qtr     3 Qtr     4 Qtr     Total
 4 =========================================================================
 5 Sales             $11500.00 $13225.00 $15208.75 $17490.06 $57423.81
 6 Labor              $5620.00  $6322.50  $7112.81  $8001.91 $27057.23
 7 Material           $2445.00  $2811.75  $3233.51  $3718.54 $12208.80
 8 Total Cost         $8065.00  $9134.25 $10346.33 $11720.45 $39266.03
 9 =========================================================================
10 Gross Profit Margin $3435.00  $4090.75  $4862.43  $5769.61 $18157.78
11 Cumulative GPM     $3435.00  $7525.75 $12388.18 $18157.78
12
13 GPM as a % of Sales   29.87%    30.93%    31.97%    32.99%    31.62%
14 -------------------------------------------------------------------------
```

8. Use the Blank command to blank the values in cells R6C2 through R7C5 by placing the cell pointer to R6C2 and typing

Keystrokes	*Results*
B	BLANK cells: R6C2
:	BLANK cells: R6C2:
Cell pointer to R7C5	BLANK cells: R6C2:R7C5
Return	Completes Blank command

9. Use the External Copy command to copy the LABOR cells (R5C2:5) of the LABOR.MP worksheet to cells R6C2 through R6C5 by positioning the cell pointer to R6C2 and typing

Keystrokes	*Results*
X	EXTERNAL: Copy List Use
C	EXTERNAL COPY from sheet: name:
LABOR.MP	EXTERNAL COPY from sheet: LABOR.MP name:
Tab LABOR	EXTERNAL COPY from sheet: LABOR.MP name: LABOR
Tab:	to: R6C2: linked:(Yes)No
Cell pointer to R6C5	to: R6C2:R6C5 linked:(Yes)No
Return	Completes External Copy command

10. Use the External Copy command to copy the MATERIAL cells (R5C2:5) of the MATERIAL.MP worksheet to cells R7C2 through R7C5 by positioning the cell pointer to R7C2 and typing

Keystrokes	*Results*
X	EXTERNAL: Copy List Use
C	EXTERNAL COPY from sheet: name:
MATERIAL.MP	EXTERNAL COPY from sheet: MATERIAL.MP name:
Tab MATERIAL	EXTERNAL COPY from sheet: MATERIAL.MP name: MATERIAL
Tab:	to: R7C2: linked:(Yes)No
Cell pointer to R7C5	to: R7C2:R7C5 linked:(Yes)No
Return	Completes External Copy command

11. The following illustration shows the results of this activity.

```
                 1             2         3         4         5         6
 1                       Product Income and Cost Analysis
 2 ----------------------------------------------------------------------
 3 Item                     1 Qtr     2 Qtr     3 Qtr     4 Qtr     Total
 4 ======================================================================
 5 Sales               $11500.00 $13225.00 $15208.75 $17490.06 $57423.81
 6 Labor                $5600.00  $5900.00  $6200.00  $6400.00 $24100.00
 7 Material             $2200.00  $2300.00  $2400.00  $2550.00  $9450.00
 8 Total Cost           $7800.00  $8200.00  $8600.00  $8950.00 $33550.00
 9 ======================================================================
10 Gross Profit Margin  $3700.00  $5025.00  $6608.75  $8540.06 $23873.81
11 Cumulative GPM       $3700.00  $8725.00 $15333.75 $23873.81
12
13 GPM as a % of Sales    32.17%    38.00%    43.45%    48.83%    41.57%
14 ----------------------------------------------------------------------
```

12. Use the External List command to check which worksheets are linked as supporting worksheets to the GPM.MP worksheet by typing

Keystrokes	*Results*
X	EXTERNAL: Copy Use List
L	Sheets supporting GPM.MP LABOR.MP MATERIAL.MP No sheets depend on GPM.MP
Return	Completes External List Command

13. Quit without saving by typing **Q N**; the operating system prompt is displayed.

Appendix A
MULTIPLAN COMMANDS

This appendix presents a directory of Multiplan commands. In addition to the main Multiplan command, subordinate commands, displayed prompts, and a brief description of the purpose of each are included. For more information about a command or prompt or to see an example, refer to the appropriate module.

Multiplan's command line is shown below. It is the starting point for all activity.

```
COMMAND:Alpha Blank Copy Delete Edit Format Goto Help Insert Lock Move
        Name Options Print Quit Sort Transfer Value Window Xternal
Select option or type command letter
```

Table A-1 Multiplan Command Structure

Command	*Display and Description*

ALPHA

ALPHA:_

Enter text (no double quotes)

Allows entry of text, rules, and other textlike information.

BLANK

BLANK cells: RnCn

Enter reference to cell or group of cells

Blanks contents of specified cell or continuous range of cells. Range is specified by typing a colon between the beginning and ending cells in the form RnCn:RnCn.

COPY

COPY: Right Down From

Select option or type command letter

Copies cell or range of cells to the right or down from the current cell position, or into current cell from another. If From option is used with a range, the range begins at the current cell position. Options include:

Table A-1 Multiplan Command Structure (Continued)

Command	*Display and Description*

Right

COPY RIGHT number of cells: starting at: RnCn

Enter a number

Down

COPY DOWN number of cells: starting at: RnCn

Enter a number

From

COPY FROM cells: RnCn to cells: RnCn

Enter reference to cell or group of cells

DELETE

DELETE: Row Column

Select option or type command letter

Deletes one or more specified rows or columns. Options include:

Row

DELETE ROW # of rows: 1 starting at: 1
between columns: 1 and: 255
Enter a number

Column

DELETE COLUMN # of columns: 1 starting at: 1
between rows: 1 and: 4095

EDIT

EDIT : R[-2]C + R[-1]C (Typical value or formula display.)

Enter a formula

EDIT : "Grand Total" (Text must be enclosed in quotes.)

Enter a formula

Used to change contents of current cell; text entries are enclosed in quotes. Use Char Right and Word Right and Char Left and Word Left to move cursor on text line. (Don't use cursor Arrow keys.)

FORMAT

FORMAT: Cells Default Options Width

Select option or type command letter

Table A-1 Multiplan Command Structure (Continued)

Command	*Display and Description*

Changes the way information is displayed in a cell. Converts numbers to dollars, percentages, decimals, etc. Positions cell contents left, center, or right. Changes cell widths. Options include:

Cells

FORMAT cells: RnCn alignment: (Def)Ctr Gen Left Right -
format code: (Def)Cont Exp Fix Gen Int $ * % - # of decimals: 0
Enter references to cell or group of cells

Default

FORMAT DEFAULT: Cells Width

Select option or type command letter

Default Cells

FORMAT DEFAULT CELLS alignment: Ctr Gen Left Right
format code: Cont Exp Fix(Gen)Int $ * % # of decimals: 0
Select option

Default Width

FORMAT DEFAULT width in chars: 10

Enter a number

Options

FORMAT OPTIONS commas: Yes No formulas: Yes(No)

Select option

Width

FORMAT WIDTH in chars or d(efault): d column: 1 through: 1

Enter a number, or d for default

GOTO

GOTO: Macro Name Row-col Window

Select option or type command letter

Jumps cell pointer to designated cell or window by cell name, row-column designation, or window number. Options include:

Macro

GOTO macro:

Enter reference to cell or group of cells

Causes named macro to operate. This is an alternative to press **Alt-nn**, where nn is the macro key code.

Table A-1 Multiplan Command Structure (Continued)

Command	Display and Description

Name

GOTO name:

Enter reference to cell or group of cells

Row-col

GOTO row: n   column: n

Enter a number

Window

GOTO WINDOW window number: n   row: n   column: n

Enter a number

HELP

Displays Multiplan help information. General help information may be displayed from the command line. Specific command help can be displayed by pressing a question mark "?" during command operation. The following information is displayed when Help is called from the command line.

```
There are three ways to use HELP:

1.  You may press the "?" key at any time during your work. The help
    text that appears will apply to the command you were using when
    you pressed "?". When you resume (by pressing "R"), your work will
    be exactly as you left it.
2.  You may view information on special topics right now by selecting
    one of the topics listed at the bottom of the screen. Type the
    first letter of the desired word.
3.  You may familiarize yourself with all the available information by
    paging through the help text right now. Select "Next" (press "N")
    "Previous" or "Start" page.

If you need information on a specific command, highlight the command name
on the proper menu (using the space bar) and press "?".

Applications

The following table provides an index to the commands and help


HELP: Resume Start Next Previous
      Applications Commands Editing Formulas Keyboard Macro
Select option or type command letter
```

Table A-1 Multiplan Command Structure (Continued)

Command	Display and Description

INSERT

INSERT: Row Column

Select option or type command letter
RnCn Cell Contents 99% Free Multiplan: Filename

Inserts one or more blank rows or columns before designated row or column. Options include:

Row

INSERT ROW # of rows: n before row: n
between columns: 1 and: 255
Enter number

Column

INSERT COLUMN # of columns: n before column: n
between rows: 1 and: 4095
Enter number

LOCK

LOCK: Cells Formulas

Select option or type command letter
RnCn Cell Contents 99% Free Multiplan: Filename

Locks (or protects) contents of one or more cells. Generally used to protect a formula from being accidentally replaced with a numerical entry. Options include:

Cells

LOCK cells: RnCn status: Locked(Unlocked)

Enter reference to cell or group of cells

Formulas

LOCK FORMULAS:

Enter Y to confirm

MOVE

MOVE: Row Column

Select option or type command letter

Moves one or more rows or columns before a selected row or column. Options include:

Row

MOVE ROW from row: n to before row: n # of rows: 1

Enter a number

Table A-1 Multiplan Command Structure (Continued)

Command	Display and Description

Column

MOVE COLUMN from column: n   to left of column: n   # of columns: 1

Enter a number

NAME

NAME: define name: to refer to: R18C6
macro: Yes(No)   command key(s):
Enter name

Lets you assign a name to a cell, range of cells, or macro. A cell might be named "Total" or "Column 3 Subtotal." The Name function also lets you assign a command key code that is used with the **Alt** key to call the macro instruction into operation. See Module 16 for additional information about macros and the Name function.

OPTIONS

OPTIONS recalc: Yes No   mute: Yes(No)
iterations: Yes(No)   completion test at:
Select option

The recalc option turns automatic recalculation off and on. When it is off, delays due to recalculation during data entry are eliminated. The mute option toggles your computer's speaker on/off when entry errors occur. The iterations and completion test options work together. When iteration is "Yes," iteration-type calculations can be made. A cell designation is entered after "completion test at:" that contains the ITERCNT( ) (iteration count) statement, which limits the number of iterations.

PRINT

PRINT: Printer File Margins Options

Select option or type command letter

Prints contents of worksheet or writes the worksheet to a disk file. Margins and Options provide for worksheet size and formatting.

File

PRINT on file:

Enter a filename

Margins

PRINT MARGINS: left: 5   top: 6   print width: 70   print length: 54
page length: 66
Enter a number

Table A-1 Multiplan Command Structure (Continued)

Command	*Display and Description*

Options

PRINT OPTIONS: area: R1:4095 setup:
formulas: Yes(No) row-col numbers: Yes(No)

The area option is used to select a range of cells for printing. The setup option allows the entry of special print codes to control printer operation. Compressed print can be controlled by entering ^ O (for Ctrl-O, the equivalent of an S1 or decimal 15). Other control codes are determined by reading your printer manual.

QUIT

QUIT:

Enter Y to save edits, N to lose edits, or cancel

Quits Multiplan session. Be sure your worksheet is saved by using Transfer-Save before quitting. If an edited worksheet has not been saved, Multiplan gives you the opportunity to type **Y** to save edits or **N** to quit without saving. If the current version of the worksheet is already saved, typing **Q** for Quit takes you directly to DOS.

SORT

SORT by column: 1 between rows: 1 and: 4095 order:(>)<

Enter number

Sorts specified column alphanumerically between designated rows. The sort is in either ascending (>) or descending order, where ascending is 0 to 9 or A to Z.

TRANSFER

TRANSFER: Load Save Clear Delete Options Rename

Select option or type command letter

Lets you control Multiplan file operations, such as loading and saving worksheets, clearing the displayed worksheet, deleting a worksheet, formatting worksheets prior to filing, and renaming a worksheet during the filing process.

Load

TRANSFER LOAD filename:

Enter a filename, or use direction keys to view directory

Save

TRANSFER SAVE filename: FILENAME

Enter a filename

Clear

TRANSFER CLEAR:

Enter Y to confirm

Used to clear displayed worksheet in preparation for either loading another worksheet or creating a new one.

Table A-1 Multiplan Command Structure (Continued)

Command	Display and Description

Delete

TRANSFER DELETE filename:

Enter a filename, or use direction keys to view directory

Options

TRANSFER OPTIONS mode: Normal Symbolic Other setup:

Select option

The Normal option saves and loads standard Multiplan files. The Symbolic format allows interchange of worksheet files with other programs, in SYLK (SYmbolic LinK) format. The Other option lets you load Lotus 1-2-3, Lotus Symphony, and VisiCalc worksheets into Multiplan. The Multiplan 2.0 CONVERTD program lets you process data from dBASE II and columnar text files for use with Multiplan. You can also use the Other mode to save 1-2-3 worksheets as long as the file name has a .WKS extension. The setup option allows you to select another drive as the default drive to which files are saved or from which they are loaded. Assuming that Multiplan is on the diskette in drive A, a common response to setup would be B: or C: for disk drive B or C.

Rename

TRANSFER RENAME filename: FILENAME

Enter a filename

Lets you rename and save the active worksheet file.

VALUE

VALUE:

Enter a formula

Lets you type a number or formula from the keyboard. This command is started automatically by typing a number or pressing the =, +, −, or (keys.

WINDOW

WINDOW: Split Border Close Link Paint

Select option or type command letter

Lets you divide the worksheet display into horizontal and vertical "windows" so that you can see different parts of a large worksheet simultaneously. For example, you may wish to see the rows containing column row headings and totals at the same time. This command also lets you draw borders around window sections, close (eliminate) windows, and link windows so that data within adjacent windows scrolls in unison.

Split

WINDOW SPLIT: Horizontal Vertical Titles

Select option or type command letter

Table A-1 Multiplan Command Structure (Continued)

Command	*Display and Description*

Horizontal

WINDOW SPLIT HORIZONTAL at row: 1 linked: Yes(No)

Enter a number

Vertical

WINDOW SPLIT VERTICAL at column: 1 linked: Yes(No)

Enter a number

Titles

WINDOW SPLIT TITLES: # of rows: 2 # of columns: 1

Enter a number

Separates (splits) row and column headings from main body of worksheet so that you can see this information while moving the cell pointer into cells that are normally off the screen.

Border

WINDOW change border in window number: 1

Enter a number

Close

WINDOW CLOSE window number: 2

Enter a number

This command eliminates (closes) the designated window, which merges the information back with the next lower-numbered window.

Link

WINDOW LINK window number: 1 with window number: 2 linked: Yes(No)

Enter a number

This command links cells in adjoining windows so that when cells are scrolled in one window, cells in the adjacent window move in unison.

Paint

WINDOW PAINT foreground: 7 background: 0 border: 7

Enter color number or use direction keys to select color

Lets you select colors for the foreground text, background, and window border. The numbers 0-15 correspond to colors on the IBM-PC and PCjr. They are:

0	black	4	red	8	bright black	12	bright red
1	blue	5	violet	9	bright blue	13	bright violet
2	green	6	yellow	10	bright green	14	bright yellow
3	cyan	7	white	11	bright cyan	15	bright white

Table A-1 Multiplan Command Structure (Continued)

Command	Display and Description

XTERNAL

EXTERNAL: Copy List Total Use

Select option or type command letter

Lets you extract cell contents from another worksheet into the one in use. Also lets you establish relationships between worksheets, so that they support each other.

Copy

EXTERNAL COPY from sheet: name:
to: RnCn linked: (Yes)No

Enter a filename

Lets you extract cell contents from named worksheet and cell to RnCn of the displayed worksheet. Linking establishes a functional relationship between the two worksheets.

List

The List option displays the following information, depending on the worksheet relationships in effect.

Relationship 1 - Supporting Worksheet:

No sheets support (Current worksheet filename)

Sheets depending on (Current worksheet filename)

Filename list

Relationship 2 - Dependent Worksheet:

Sheets supporting (Current worksheet filename)

Filename list

No sheets depend on (Current worksheet filename)

Relationship 3 - Supporting and Dependent Worksheet:

Sheets supporting (Current worksheet filename)

Filename list

Sheets depending on (Current worksheet filename)

Filename list

Total

EXTERNAL TOTAL from sheet: name:
starting at: operation: + – * /

Enter a filename

Table A-1 Multiplan Command Structure (Continued)

Command	Display and Description
	This function is good for combining the values in a number of similar worksheets containing common sales or cost information. It lets you combine values in one or more other worksheets with the current worksheet. Worksheet names are separated by commas or entered as a range, i.e., SALES1:SALES7. Enter the name of the combined range of cells in the name field. Enter the upper left-hand cell of the range in the starting at field. The + - * / operations specify whether values are added, subtracted, multiplied, or divided.
Use	
	EXTERNAL USE filename: instead of:
	Enter filename
	Lets you change references to externally dependent worksheets by substituting a new filename for the previously linked filename.

Appendix B
MULTIPLAN MATHEMATICAL OPERATORS

Mathematical operators are used with numbers and cell positions. Cell positions are expressed as relative, absolute, or both. Logical operators are used to compare two numbers (the value of two cells or cell ranges.). A true or false value is returned when a logical comparison is made.

Appendix B-1 lists and describes Multiplan's mathematical operators, including trigonometric functions and string operators.

Table B-1 Mathematical Operators

Operator	*Description*
+	Addition operator R5C3 + R5C4 12*(R[-2]C + R[-1]C)
–	Subtraction operator RC[-1]-25
*	Multiplication operator 52*49.50 RC[-2]*RC[-1]
/	Division operator R[-3]C/52
%	Percent operator 25% (the same as 25/100)
( )	Parentheses - used within formulas for grouping.
^	Exponent operator 4 ^ 3 (Four to the third power) R3C2 ^ 2 (The contents of cell R3C2 squared)

Table B-1 Mathematical Operators

Operator	Description
:	Range operator - combines all contiguous cells within the range specified by the cell references on either side of the range operator (:). The range can be a row, a column, or a rectangular area where the cell references are at the R1C1:R20C8 R1C1:R[+ 19]C[+ 7] Union operator - combines referenced cells on an individual basis. R1C1,R1C3,R1C4 R1C1,RC[+ 2],RC[+ 3]
(Space)	Intersection operator - designates a group of intersecting cells for use with the same operator. The following formula finds the maximum value in the current row within columns C3 through C5 and column C8. MAX(R C3:C5,C8)
&	Concatentation operator - combines text strings with values. The formula "$"&"3.50" gives you "$3.50".
ABS	Returns the absolute (positive) value of a mathematical expression (formula). ABS(R3C5-R4C5)
ATAN	Returns the angle of the tangent (inverse tangent). ATAN(18)
AVERAGE	Calculates the average value of a range of cells. AVERAGE(R[-10]C:R[-1]C)
COLUMN( )	Returns the integer value of the deignated column number. The number is relative to the column position of the formula. Assume that the following formulas are entered into a cell in column 1. COLUMN( ) + 3*12 (The resulting value is 37.) (COLUMN( ) + 3)*12 (The resulting value is 48.)
COS	Returns the cosine of an angle expressed in radian form. COS(.707)
COUNT	Returns the number of numerical entries in a range of cells. COUNT(R3C4:R10C4)
EXP	Returns the inverse of the natural logarithm (e(2.7182818)). EXP(2)

Table B-1 Mathematical Operators

Operator	*Description*
INDEX	Returns the value of the designated cell within a row, column, or rectangular area. If a row has the name Totals, the expression INDEX(Totals,3) where "Totals" is an area and "3" is a subscript, returns the value of the cell in the third column of the Totals row.
INT	Returns the largest whole number (integer) less than or equal to the expression. INT(15.9) (Returns 15.)
LEN	Returns the number of characters and spaces in a text string. The expression LEN(R1C1) returns the number of characters and spaces found in cell R1C1.
LN	Returns the natural logarithm of the expression. LN(14)
LOG10	Returns the base 10 (Briggsian) logarithm of the expression. LOG10(5)
MAX	Returns the maximum value found within a range of cells or list of numbers. MAX(R[-10]C:R[-1]C)
MID	Returns one or more specified characters within a text string. The form MID("TEXT",START,CHARACTERS) is used, where "TEXT" is the text string, START is a whole number representing the starting point within the text string, and CHARACTERS represents the number of characters returned. The expression MID("FFFFFDCBAA",INT(Score/10),1) takes the value of the cell with the name "Score", divides it by 10, and converts the result to an integer (whole number). A score of 75 is converted to 7.5, which has the integer value 7. This is the starting point in the string "FFFFFDCBAA", which is C. The number 1 returns a single character, which represents the score.
MIN	Returns the minimum value found within a range of cells or list of numbers. MIN(R2C2:R20C5)
MOD	Returns the remainder of a division operation (dividend,divisor); the remainder has the same sign as the divisor. MOD(5,2) (The remainder is 1.) MOD(7,-3) (The remainder is -2.)

Table B-1 Mathematical Operators

Operator	*Description*
PI( )	Returns the value 3.1415926535898. 3*PI( )
ROW( )	Returns the integer value of the deignated row number. The number is relative to the row position of the formula. Assume that the following formulas are entered into a cell in row 10. ROW( ) + 3*12 (The resulting value is 46.) (ROW( ) + 3)*12 (The resulting value is 156.)
SIGN	Returns a number representing the algebraic sign of the designated value, where 1 is positive, 0 is zero, and -1 is negative. SIGN(R3C2)
SIN	Returns the sine of an angle expressed in radian form. SIN(.707)
SQRT	Returns the square root of a value, where the value must be positive. SQRT(R15C5)
STDEV	Returns the sample standard deviation of a list of values. STDEV(R[-11]C:R[-1]C)
SUM	Returns the sum of a list of values. SUM(R[-11]C:R[-1]C)
TAN	Returns the tangent of an angle expressed in radian form. TAN(.707)

Appendix C

MULTIPLAN LOGICAL AND BOOLEAN OPERATORS

Logical and Boolean operators, like mathematical operators, are used in combination with numeric values and cell references. Table C-1 contains a list of these operators and descriptions of each.

Table C-1 Multiplan Logical and Boolean Operators

Operator	*Description*
<	Less than operator
	R1C5 < R2C5 (This says that cell R1C5 is less than R2C5.)
< =	Less than or equal to operator
	R1C5 < = R[+ 1]C[+ 4]
=	Equal to operator
	(R[-3]C + R[-2]C) = (R[-3]C[-1] + R[-2]C[-1])
>	Greater than operator
	(AVERAGE(R[-10]C:R[-1]C)) > (MAX(R[-10]C[-1]:R[-1]C[-1]))
> =	Greater than or equal to operator
	(MIN(R[-10]C:R[-1]C)) > = (MIN(R[-10]C[-1]:R[-1]C[-1]))
< >	Not equal to operator
	R2C7 < > R3C7
IF	The following logical operators are used with the IF statement, which is entered in the form
	IF(expression, then value, else value)
	where
	expression is two or more fields containing a logical operator,
	then value is returned if the expression is true,
	else value is returned if the expression is false.
	Examples of ways in which IF is used are shown with the following logical operators.

Table C-1 Multiplan Logical and Boolean Operators (Continued)

Operator	*Description*
AND	The logical AND operator requires that all expressions within the designated cells be true to return the *then value.* **NOTE** In the following examples, cell names are used rather than absolute or relative values. Names are assigned to cells using the Name command. IF(AND(Budget > Expense,Total Income > Total Cost),"Staff OK","Reduce Staff")
DELTA( )	Used with ITERCNT( ) to display the difference between two values in an iterative (circular) computation. (See Module 19.)
FALSE( )	Used to test logical expressions during formula development; returns the logical value FALSE when testing an expression or formula.
ISERROR	("Is Error") If designated cell contains an error value, the *then value* is returned; if no error value exists, the *else value* is returned. IF(ISERROR(R3C4),"Missing Value","Setup OK")
ISNA	("Is Not Available") If designated cell does not contain the expression, returns the *then value*; otherwise, the *else value* is returned. IF(ISNA(Total), "No Total","Total")
ITERCNT( )	Limits the number of iterations ("iteration count") in a circular computation, where two or more cells are interdependent for their value. (See Module 19.)
NOT	The logical NOT operator returns the *then value* if the expression is false; otherwise, the *else value* is returned. IF(NOT(Budget > Expense),"Within Budget","Over Budget")
OR	The logical OR operator requires that one of the expressions within the designated cells be true to return the *then value.* IF(OR(Budget > Expense,Total Income > Total Cost),"Staff OK","Reduce Staff")
TRUE( )	Used to test logical expressions during formula development; returns the logical value TRUE when testing an expression or formula.

Appendix D
MULTIPLAN FINANCIAL OPERATORS

Multiplan offers a powerful assortment of financial operators. Table D-1 contains a list of these operators and corresponding descriptions of each.

Table D-1 Multiplan Financial Operators

Operator	*Description*
FV, NPER, PMT, PV, RATE, T	These financial operators work together to solve common financial problems. For example, knowing the present value (PV), annual interest rate (RATE), and number of payment periods (NPER), you can calculate the monthly payment. The operators are defined: FV Future value (value at the end of the payment period) NPER Number of payments (number of payments or deposits) PMT Periodic payment (the amount of each payment) PV Present value (amount financed) RATE Periodic interest rate (10% per year = 0.10/12 = .8333) T Time of payment 0 = end, 1 = beginning of each period. The default value of T is 0. The general forms for the equations are PMT(Rate,Periods,Present Value,Future Value,Time) FV(Rate,Periods,Payment,Present Value,Time) RATE(Periods,Payment,Present Value,Future Value,Time,Guess) PV(Rate,Periods,Payment,Future Value, Time) NPER(Rate,Payment,Present Value,Future Value,Time) The default values for FV, T, and Guess are always 0. **TIP:** Cash paid is represented as a negative value. Cash received is positive. You may use a negative present value or payment value to ensure that your answers are positive. Without the negative entry, Multiplan's financial algorithm sometimes yields an unwanted negative value or an error message. The examples show the use of a negative value to obtain the desired result.

Table D-1 Multiplan Financial Operators (Continued)

Operator	*Description*
	Examples: What is the monthly payment for a $10,000 loan having a 10% annual interest rate? (Monthly interest is .1/12 = .83333% or .008333) PMT(.008333,24,-10000) The answer is 461.45 What interest rate is required for $100,000 to double in value over a 10-year period? Interest is computed using ten 12-month periods (120 total periods). Use .017 as your guess and 0 for T. RATE(120,1000,-100000,200000,0,.017) The answer is 1.34% per month or 16.08% per year (APR). What is the future value of the amounts saved if you deposit $200 per month for 5 years and your bank gives you 7.5% annual interest rate? Assume you start with $1000 in your account. FV(0.075/12,60,-200,1000,0) The answer is $13052.13
IRR	Returns the *internal rate of return*, which is a financial derivation found within a list of cash flow values. The equation is used to find a net present value and interest rate that yields a return of zero. The form of the IRR equation is: IRR(list of values, interest rate guess) Assume that the range of cells R7C3:R7C8 list cash flow figures as follows: -$2.4 -$1.1 $0.5 $0.7 $1.5 $2.0 The formula: IRR(R3C3:R3C8,.05) yields 0.0825243 (about 8.25%) This tells you that an interest rate of 8.25% applied to the net present value generated by the cash flows in the list yields a zero rate of return. By increasing the cash flow, your interest rate increases. Decreasing the cash flow gives you a negative interest rate. This indicates a business loss or the need for additional revenues.
NPV	Calculates the net present value of the amount required to produce a cash flow at a specified interest rate. The form of the NPV operator is NPV(Rate,List) The interest rate is expressed as either a percentage or a decimal fraction. The list is a series of time periods (or intervals), where each entry is the income required at the end of each period. NPV(8.8%,R2C2:R2C6)

Appendix E
OTHER MULTIPLAN OPERATORS

Table E-1 contains a list and descriptions of miscellaneous Multiplan operators.

Table E-1 Other Multiplan Operators

Operator	*Description*
DOLLAR	Displays a value as dollars and cents. DOLLAR(SUM(R[-5]C:R[-1]C)) or DOLLAR(12.95)
FIXED	Displays a value as a fixed-place decimal fraction. FIXED(R3C2/R4C2,2) This expression fixes the results of R3C2 divided by R4C2 to two decimal places.
LOOKUP	This operator is used with tables of numbers, such as tax tables or rate tables, where a value that corresponds to a number is returned. Several Lookup expressions can be used in combination to return a computed number. The LOOKUP operator is described in Module 15 of this book.
REPT	Repeats the specified text a given number of times. The form of this operator is REPT("TEXT",NUMBER) where "TEXT" is a character and NUMBER is the number of times the character is to be repeated. If you want to draw a row of 12 asterisks, the expression REPT("*",12) is used. The NUMBER can be a cell designation or a formula.
ROUND	Rounds a value to a specified number of digits. The form of this operator is ROUND(NUMBER,DIGITS) where NUMBER is a numerical value and DIGITS is the number of decimal places. The expression ROUND(R3C5/1.667,2) rounds the contents of cell R3C5 divided by 1.667 to two places.
VALUE	Converts a number entered as text to its numerical value. The expression VALUE(RC[-6]) where the content of the designated cell is "15" entered as text, evaluates the expression as a number.

Appendix F
MULTIPLAN ERROR MESSAGES

Multiplan displays a number of descriptive error messages, or error values. These messages tell you what to look for, which is helpful in knowing how to remedy worksheet problems. A list of error messages and descriptions of each is contained in Table F-1.

Table F-1 Error Messages

Message	*Description/Cause*
#DIV/0	Divide by zero error. The cell contains a formula that uses a dividend that is presently set to zero.
#NAME?	The cell referenced for a name (or label) is empty. Either the cell reference is wrong or text within the cell is missing.
#N/A	One or more values are not available to complete a computation.
#NULL!	Indicates discontinuity in a specified series of cells. Similar to no (null) value or a missing union (,) symbol.
#NUM!	The number is too large or too small or the illegal use of an arithmetic function exists.
#REF!	Relative reference missing, as when a cell value within a deleted area is specified in a formula.
#VALUE!	Indicates that a number is used in place of text, text is used in place of a number, or a reference is given instead of a value.

Appendix G

MULTIPLAN CONTROL KEYS FOR DIFFERENT TERMINALS AND COMPUTERS

(ALPHABETIZED BY MANUFACTURER)

ADM-3A, ADM-5

Backspace	Ctrl-U
Select previous item on menu	Ctrl-U
Character Left	Ctrl-V
Character Right	Ctrl-B

Altos II

Next Window	F1
Next Unlocked Cell	F2
Home	Home
Page Up	PREV PAGE
Page Down	NEXT PAGE
Page Left	F5
Page Right	F6
Cancel	ESC
Help	HELP
Delete	Del LINE, Del CHAR
Character Left	F13
Character Right	F14
Word Left	F15
Word Right	F16
Recalculate	F3
Reference	F4

Burroughs ET-2000

Cancel	ESC
Character Left	F1
Character Right	F2
Word Left	F3
Word Right	F4
Reference	F7
Help	HELP,F10
Next Window	F6
Next Unlocked cell	F5
Recalculate	F8
Home	Home,CLR
End	F9
Page Up	BACK
Page Down	NEXT
Page Right	6 (on keypad)
Page Left	4 (on keypad)

Columbia, Compaq, and Corona (See IBM)

Datavue 132/C

Backspace	Ctrl-U
Next Window	F6
Next Unlocked Cell	F7
Page Up	F13
Page Down	F14
Page Left	F12
Page Right	F15
Cancel	ESC
Help	F8
Recalculate	F10
Delete	F3
Character Left	F2
Character Right	F4
Word Left	F1
Word Right	F5
Reference	F9

DEC Rainbow 100

Cancel	CANCEL
Return,Enter	DO
Character Left	PF1
Character Right	PF2
Word Left	PF3
Word Right	PF4
Reference	F17
Help	HELP
Next Window	F19
Next Unlocked cell	FIND
Recalculate	F18
Home	MAIN SCREEN
End	EXIT
Page Up	PREV SCREEN
Page Down	NEXT SCREEN
Page Right	INSERT HERE
Page Left	REMOVE

DEC VT100

Character Left	PF1
Character Right	PF2
Word Left	PF3
Word Right	PF4

Dynalogic Hyperion

Cancel	Esc
Home	Home
End	End
Next Unlocked cell	F1
Change Window	F2
Character Left	F6
Character Right	F7
Word Left	F8
Word Right	F9
Delete	Del
Page Up	Pg Up
Page Down	Pg Dn
Recalculate	F3
Reference	F4
Help	F10

Eagle 1600 Personal Computer

Next Window	F5
Next Unlocked Cell	F6
Home	Home, TOP (F7)
End	END (F8)
Page Up	F16
Page Left	F17
Page Right	F18
Page Down	F19
Cancel	ESCAPE
Help	HELP
Recalculate	F9
Backspace	INS, F15
Character Left	F1
Character Right	F2
Word Left	F3
Word Right	F4
Reference	F10

Eagle Spirit (See IBM)

Ericsson PC (See IBM)

Grid Compass

Cancel	ESC
Delete	Code-Delete
Character Left	F9, Shift-Left Arrow
Character Right	F10, Shift-Right Arrow
Word Left	F7, Code-Shift-Left Arrow
Word Right	F8, Code-Shift-Right Arrow
Help	Code-?
Next Window	F1
Next Unlocked Cell	F2
Reference	F3
Recalculate	F4
Home	F5, Code-Shift-Up Arrow
End	F6, Code-Shift-Down Arrow
Page Up	Code-Up Arrow
Page Down	Code-Down Arrow
Page Right	Code-Right Arrow
Page Left	Code-Left Arrow

Hazeltine Esprit

Backspace	Ctrl-U
Select previous item on menu	Ctrl-U
Word Left	Ctrl-V
Word Right	Ctrl-B

Heath/Zenith H19 (Use Shift with keypad entries)

Character Left	IC (keypad 7)
Character Right	DC (keypad 9)
Word Left	IL (keypad 1)

Word Right	DL (keypad 3)
Page Up	F1
Page Down	F2
Page Left	F3
Page Right	F4
End	F5
Cancel	ERASE
Help	RED
Recalculate	BLUE
Reference	WHITE

Honeywell Microsystem 6/10

Cancel	Esc
Delete	Delete
Character Left	F1
Character Right	F2
Word Left	F3
Word Right	F4
Reference	F7
Help	F10
Next Window	F6
Next Unlocked Cell	F5
Recalculate	F8
Home	Home
End	End
Page Up	Page Up
Page Down	Page Down
Page Right	F11
Page Left	F12

IBM PC,XT,AT and Compatibles

Next Window	F1
Next Unlocked Cell	F2
Page Up	PgUp
Page Down	PgDn
Page Left	Ctrl-left arrow
Page Right	Ctrl-right arrow
Home	Home
Home Window	Ctrl-Home
End	End
Cancel	Esc
Help	Alt-H
Recalculate	F4
Character Left	F9
Character Right	F10
Word Left	F7
Word Right	F8
Reference	F3
Extend Key (:)	F6
Single Step	Shift-F5
Edit Macro	F5

ITT Xtra (See IBM)

Olivetti M20 L1 (ANSI Mode)

Character Left	Command-1
Character Right	Command-2
Word Left	Command-3
Word Right	Command-4
Page Up	Command-5
Page Down	Command-6
Page Left	Command-7
Page Right	Command-8
Delete	Command-9
Help	Command-0

Sanyo (See IBM)

Televideo 910/912/920

Backspace	Ctrl-U
Select previous item on menu	Ctrl-U
Character Left	Ctrl-V
Character Right	Ctrl-B

Televideo 910 +

Backspace	Ctrl-B
Select previous item on menu	Ctrl-B
Character Left	Ctrl-U
Character Right	Ctrl-\

Televideo 925, 950, and TS-1603

Next Unlocked Cell	F6
Page Up	F8
Page Down	F7
Page Left	F9
Page Right	F10
Cancel	F1
Backspace	Ctrl-B
Select previous item on menu	Ctrl-B
Help	F11
Character Left	F2, Ctrl-U
Character Right	F3, Ctrl-J
Word Left	F4
Word Right	F5

Texas Instruments Professional Computer

Next Window	F6
Next Unlocked Cell	F5
Page Up	ALT + up arrow
Page Down	ALT + down arrow
Page Left	ALT + left arrow
Page Right	ALT + right arrow
End	F9
Cancel	ESC
Help	F10
Recalculate	F8
Character Left	F1
Character Right	F2
Word Left	F3
Word Right	F4
Reference	F7

Wang Professional Computer

Cancel	CANCEL
Return,Enter	EXEC
Character Left	FORMAT
Character Right	MERGE
Word Left	NOTE
Word Right	STOP
Reference	SRCH
Help	HELP
Next Window	GO TO
Next Unlocked Cell	COMMAND
Recalculate	MOVE
Home	Home
End	Super/Subscript Key
Page Up	PREV, INDENT
Page Down	NEXT, PAGE
Page Right	DECTAB
Page Left	CENTER

Zenith H19 (see Heath/Zenith H19)

Zenith Z100

Next Window	F10
Next Unlocked Cell	F11, LINEFEED
Page Up	F8, Shift + up arrow
Page Down	F7, Shift + down arrow
Page Left	F6, Shift + right arrow
Page Right	F1, Shift + left arrow
End	F9
Cancel	Esc
Help	HELP
Character Left	F3
Character Right	F4
Word Left	F2
Word Right	F5
Reference	F12

Appendix H
MULTIPLAN EXERCISES

1. *About This Book*

   a. Where can electronic worksheets be used?
   b. How might you use the examples in this book?
   c. Where can Multiplan operators be found in this book?
   d. Name three computers that use Multiplan.
   e. What should you know before learning Multiplan?

2. *Multiplan Overview and Sample Session*

   a. Describe the organization of a typical worksheet.
   b. What is a *cell*?
   c. Describe the meaning of R3C8.
   d. How large is the Multiplan worksheet?
   e. What kind of information may be entered into a cell?
   f. What is an absolute cell reference?
   g. What is a relative cell reference?
   h. Write the relative cell reference for a cell two rows up and one column to the left.
   i. Write a list of function keys on your computer and describe their use.
   j. What key lets you "undo" entries if you goof?

3. *Multiplan Command Structure and Operators*

   a. Describe the Multiplan command line and how it is used.
   b. What information is available on the status line?
   c. What is meant by the *cell pointer*?
   d. Describe the meaning of a subordinate choice of a command and give an example
   e. Where are mathematical and logical operators used?
   f. Write the symbols for add, subtract, multiply, and divide.
   g. What is the difference between a range operator and a union operator?
   h. Write six logical operator symbols and give their meaning.
   i. What is an error message?
   j. Why would you want to merge a worksheet into a word processed document?

4. *Recommended Learning Sequence*

   a. What is the purpose of the recommended learning sequence?
   b. What is the advantage of learning by doing?
   c. Which Module should you read first when beginning the learning sequence?

5. *Alpha*

   a. What is the primary purpose of the Alpha command?
   b. What should you do if you make an entry error?
   c. Describe two ways to start commands.
   d. What key is pressed to complete a command?
   e. What keys are used to move the cursor on the command line?
   f. When are double quotes used for text entry?
   g. What can be used for a horizontal rule?

6. *Blank*

   a. Describe the purpose of the Blank command.
   b. How many cells may be simultaneously blanked? Explain.
   c. Write a Blank cells reference that uses the range and union operators.
   d. How can Multiplan be used as a desktop calculator?

7. *Copy*

   a. Describe the use of the Copy command.
   b. What is the difference between copy from and copy right?
   c. Write the keystrokes and results for copying a cell six cells to the right with the cell pointer at cell R4C4.
   d. Write the keystrokes and results for copying cells R3C1:R3C4 to cells R5C1:R5C4. (Tip: Use Copy From.)
   e. Describe three benefits offered by the Copy command.

8. *Delete*

   a. Describe the purpose of the Delete command.
   b. How large of an area may be deleted?
   c. Write the keystrokes and results for deleting rows 5 and 6.
   d. Write the keystrokes and results for deleting column 8.
   e. Write the keystrokes and results to delete a square cell area in rows 2 and 3 and columns 4 and 5.
   f. What happens to relative and absolute cell references within formulas when cell positions change as a result of deletion?

9. *Edit*

   a. Describe the purpose of the Edit command?
   b. How might you change a cell's contents without using the Edit command?
   c. List the keys used for cursor control and deletion during Edit.
   d. What must surround Alpha entries before completing an edit?

10. *Format*

   a. Describe two uses of the Format command.
   b. What are the four selections offered by the Format command?
   c. Write the keystrokes and results for centering text in cells R2C3 through R2C6.
   d. Write the keystrokes and results for displaying a number in cell R5C4 as dollars and cents.
   e. Write the keystrokes and results for displaying the numbers in cells R3C6 through R9C6 as percent to two decimal places.
   f. What is the primary purpose of the Format Default command?
   g. Write the keystrokes and results to change the width of columns 2 through 5 to five spaces.

11. *Goto*

   a. What is meant by "jumping" the cursor?
   b. Describe two ways to designate a cell position with the Goto command.
   c. Write the keystrokes and results used to move the cell pointer from window 2 to window 1.

12. *Help*

   a. How is the Help command activated from the command line?
   b. How can help information be displayed while a command is in progress?
   c. Describe the method used to display the next screen of help information.
   d. Describe how you might display help information about your keyboard.

13. *Insert*

   a. Describe the purpose of the Insert command.
   b. Write the keystrokes and results for inserting a row before row 3.
   c. Write the keystrokes and results for inserting a column before column 4.
   d. Write the keystrokes and results for inserting two cells in row 3 between columns 4 and 5.
   e. What happens to absolute and relative cell references within formulas that are affected by cell insertion?

14. *Lock*

   a. What is another word for *lock*?
   b. What type of cells are affected by the Lock command?
   c. Write the keystrokes and results for locking cell R8C4.
   d. Write the keystrokes and results for unlocking cell R7C3.
   e. Write the keystrokes and results for locking all formulas and text entries.
   f. How can you determine which cells are locked?
   g. What is meant by *next unlocked cell*?

15. *Lookup*

   a. What is *looked up* in a lookup table?
   b. What is returned from a lookup table?
   c. How may several values be extracted from a lookup table?
   d. Name three typical lookup table applications.

16. *Macro*

   a. Define the term *macro*.
   b. Describe an advantage of a macro.
   c. What function is used to type a macro?
   d. Write the three steps in macro creation.
   e. Make a list of six macro control functions and their meaning.

17. *Move*

   a. How does the Move command differ from the Copy command?
   b. What may be moved?
   c. Write the keystrokes and results for moving row 5 to before row 11.
   d. Write the keystrokes and results for moving columns 2 and 3 to the left of column 6.
   e. What happens to absolute and relative cell references within formulas that are affected by moving rows or columns?

18. *Name*

   a. What is the purpose of the Name command?
   b. Why would you want to name a series of cells?
   c. What is used between words in a name?
   d. Write the keystrokes and results for assigning the name "Subtotals" to columns 3 through 6 of row 5.
   e. What happens to a formula that references a named cell when it is relocated by the Insert Row command?

19. *Options*

    a. What three functions are performed by the Options command?
    b. Explain why you might want to turn off automatic recalculation.
    c. Write the keystrokes and results for turning off automatic recalculation.
    d. What key is used to cause recalculation?
    e. What is the purpose of the Options Mute command?
    f. What is an *iterative formula*?
    g. What is the purpose of the ITERCNT( ) operator?
    h. What does the DELTA( ) operator evaluate?

20. *Print*

    a. Where can files be printed?
    b. What are the selections offered by the Print command?
    c. Write the keystrokes to print a file with the default options and margins.
    d. Write the keystrokes used to print a document to a file named TEXT setup as follows:
       Left margin of 10
       Print width of 60
       Area: columns 1 through 5 of rows 1 through 20
       Row-col numbers (Yes)
    e. What is the purpose of the Print Options Setup selection?

21. *Quit*

    a. What is the purpose of the Quit command?
    b. What step should be taken prior to quitting?
    c. Why is "Enter Y to confirm" displayed?
    d. What is displayed after pressing Y to confirm?

22. *Sort*

    a. Describe the purpose of the Sort command.
    b. Define the terms *ascending* and *descending*.
    c. What is a *multiple sort*?
    d. Write the keystrokes and results for sorting the cells in column 3 between rows 5 and 25.
    e. Describe an application of the Sort command.

23. *Transfer*

    a. What is the general purpose of the Transfer command?
    b. How can a disk file directory by viewed with the Transfer command?
    c. Describe the purpose of the Transfer Load command.

d. Describe the procedure for loading a Lotus 1-2-3 worksheet into Multiplan.
e. Write the keystrokes and results used for saving a new worksheet as ANALYSIS.MP.
f. What is meant by *overwriting* an existing file?
g. Describe the purpose of the following commands:
   (1) Transfer Rename
   (2) Transfer Delete
   (3) Transfer Options Mode
   (4) Transfer Options Setup

24. *Value*

a. What type of information is entered using the Value command?
b. Describe three ways to start the Value command.
c. What is a formula?
d. Write a formula that sums all numbers in column 5 between rows 2 and 12 with the cell pointer located at R13C5.

25. *Window*

a. What is a *window*?
b. What are the five selections available in the Window command?
c. How is the cell pointer moved from one window to another?
d. What is the purpose of the Window Split Titles command?
e. What is a window border?
f. How may a window be eliminated?
g. What is the effect of linking windows?
h. How may window linking be checked?
i. How are the cursor keys used to change screen colors?

26. *Xternal (or External)*

a. What is the primary purpose of the External command?
b. Write the keystrokes used to copy the value from a cell named "Total" in an external worksheet named COST.MP.
c. How may you determine supporting and dependent worksheets?
d. Write the keystrokes and results for changing the name of an externally linked worksheet form 84COST.MP to 85COST.MP.
e. Describe a typical application for the External command.
f. How is an external worksheet link dissolved?

Index

THE ILLUSTRATED SERIES

WPI's Popular Computer Books
• Learning • Teaching • Reference

The Illustrated WordStar Book and every Illustrated Book provides:

- A Recommended Learning Sequence for beginners
- Practical Exercises to check your progress
- Hundreds of sample illustrated examples
- Modules (chapters) arranged alphabetically
- A complete reference glossary

0-915381-83-4

Millions of WordStar users now have the power of an Illustrated Series book for the most popular word processing package available!

THE ILLUSTRATED WORDSTAR BOOK

• WordStar • MailMerge • SpellStar • CorrectStar

RUSSELL A. STULTZ

This book is a perfect mate to the MicroPro WordStar Professional series of programs. Numerous illustrated examples show how to use WordStar, MailMerge, SpellStar, and CorrectStar. Helpful tips are included for WordStar installation and customization.

THE ILLUSTRATED MS/PC-DOS® BOOK

RUSSELL A. STULTZ

"a valuable introductory text . . . one of those rare finds."

- John McGinty, DALTRUG

0-915381-53-2

This reference/tutorial tells you how to maximize the power of MS/PC-DOS, the premier operating system on the market today. The book provides tips on batch files, system prompts, special commands and functions in brief, easy-to-understand modules (chapters). Illustrated examples explain even the most complex DOS functions. DOS versions 1.10 through 3.00 are described to help owners of the IBM PC, PC/XT, PC/AT, PCjr, TIPC, and PC compatibles.

VISIT YOUR LOCAL BOOK STORE TODAY!
If these books are not available, contact Wordware Publishing, Inc.

CALL TOLL FREE 1-800-231-7467